Happy Birthday
to Jim

Chuck Thompson
HOF "93"

11 Dec 96

Ain't the Beer Cold!

Ain't the Beer Cold!

BY HALL-OF-FAMER
CHUCK THOMPSON

with Gordon Beard

Diamond Communications, Inc.
South Bend, Indiana
1996

Ain't the Beer Cold!

Copyright © 1996 by Chuck Thompson

10 9 8 7 6 5 4 3 2 1

Manufactured in the United States of America

Diamond Communications, Inc.
Post Office Box 88
South Bend, Indiana 46624
(219) 299-9278
Fax: (219) 299-9296
Orders only: 1-800-480-3717

Library of Congress Cataloging-in-Publication Data

Thompson, Chuck, 1921–
    Ain't the beer cold! / by Hall-of-Famer Chuck Thompson
with Gordon Beard.
       p.   cm.
    ISBN 1-888698-01-2
    1. Thompson, Chuck, 1921– . 2. Sportscasters--United
States--Biography. 3. Baltimore Orioles (Baseball team)--History.
I. Beard, Gordon, 1926– . II. Title.
GV742.42.T56A3 1996
070.4'49796'092--dc20   96-30428
   [B]   CIP

Contents

Acknowledgments

Paraphrasing that noted jock philosopher Yogi Berra, I'd like to thank some of those who made this book necessary.

Many thanks to my wife Joan, who has been supportive throughout our 20 years of marriage despite having only a minimal interest in my career of covering sports. I hope she finds this approach to the athletes more to her liking.

Bob Brown, who joined the Orioles about the time I started covering the team, provided invaluable answers to my baseball questions and honed my writing efforts with insightful editing. He played a major role in my rehabilitation after a life-threatening illness in 1992 by providing writing and editing assignments with several publications. It's been my good fortune to have been associated with such a dedicated professional, who remains a friend even though he remains a taskmaster.

Baltimore Sun sports columnist John Steadman, once my high school baseball opponent, was a natural source for answers to my questions about football. He's a walking encyclopedia on the Baltimore Colts and the National Football League. I also depended on Fred Rasmussen of the *Sun*, whom I consider my own personal tracer of obscure information.

Also, kudos to Orioles traveling secretary Phil Itzoe for clarifying a couple of stories and to Monica Windley and Thom Keenan of the Orioles who helped locate some old photographs.

Lastly, it was truly a pleasure to be regaled by Chuck Thompson as he relived the memories of a colorful career. I felt as though I shared in his life experiences and hope that I've been able to transfer those feelings to the printed page.

Gordon Beard

To my dad, L.S. Thompson, a man of courage, honor, and intelligence who commanded respect from all who knew him.

To Harold Cupp, my brother-in-law, for his courage in the valiant fight against diabetes.

And to the athletes, without whom there would be no book.

Preface

To the reader: if you are a baseball or football fan who loves the foundation of those sports—statistics—this may not be a book for you. But if the golden memories of the past are still alive in you, this book may help you understand the personalities of those who performed on the playing field.

The stories about the author you read at your own risk.

C.T.

Chapter 1

Destiny, Fate, or Good Fortune?

The travel time between my a-dopted hometown of Reading, Pennsylvania, and Cooperstown, New York, is less than a day on the highway.

But it took me 54 years to reach the National Baseball Hall of Fame, and then only with the help of a lot of good friends—the men and women who taught me my profession, my peers in the broadcast booths, and, most of all, that vast audience who encouraged, supported, and listened to me through all those years.

As a high school graduate in 1939, I entered the workaday world at a most inopportune time—in the midst of a lingering depression and on the eve of World War II.

My future was uncertain, at best, but I compounded the already foggy outlook because I had no special training and absolutely no idea of what kind of job I would seek.

My dad was in the insurance business, a power plant specialist, so he may have tried to lead me in that direction. He also had been a policeman, and, as a deputy sheriff, was still escorting prisoners until age 84. Police work, therefore, was another possibility. Meanwhile, as I was pondering my future, I was marking time as a dance band vocalist, singing popular ballads of the day like "Deep Purple," "Who?," and "Marie."

In my senior year at Reading High School, I took a college

preparatory course that was heavy on English. Near the end of the end of the year, the teacher asked everyone how he or she intended to apply what was learned in the course.

Student after student stood up and said things like, "I think I'm going to college at Bucknell," or "I'm going to Albright in the fall."

The survey was done alphabetically, so I was one of the last called.

"I really don't have any idea," was my frank response, one that clearly was not expected by Miss Runyeon and obviously caused her some consternation. "I haven't given it any thought."

"Then, why in the world did you take the course?" she inquired.

"Because all my friends did."

"Well, Mr. Thompson," she said kind of whimsically while measuring her words for emphasis, "I hope that in the coming years, we won't find you leaning on a shovel somewhere." The class erupted with laughter.

The following fall, Miss Runyeon came to the studio of radio station WEEU with her drama club, to present a skit. And, who do think was the announcer who put the show on the air and took it off? You guessed it, none other than yours truly, indecisive Chuck.

Miss Runyeon walked into the studio with the students, saw me, gave a curt little nod, and started walking around the room as she studied each of the four corners with more than cursory attention.

At the conclusion of her mini-tour, she finally spoke her first words: "Mr. Thompson, I can't seem to find a shovel anywhere."

We both laughed and hugged one another, and Miss Runyeon was tickled to death for me. I don't think I ever saw her again, but she and my other teachers had a great influence on me.

My sudden landing of a job certainly wasn't the result of anything I meticulously planned. Rather, it was the result of a simple dare from Jean Guilden, a neighbor from around the corner on Perkiomen Avenue who lived next door to Paul Breedy, the program director at radio station WRAW.

Jean approached me on a night when I was singing for Joe

Destiny, Fate, or Good Fortune?

Lombardo's band, which had been around about six years before I joined it. Jean and I had known each other for sometime and, apparently taken by my voice, she suggested I give some thought to getting into radio. I told her I didn't think too much of that idea.

But Jean said the station was looking for someone, and suggested that I was actually *afraid* to audition. Now, that was a challenge, and shed a new light on the discussion. One word led to another and finally Jean said, "If I set up the audition, will you go?"

"You're darn right!"

At the station, the program director asked me to read some commercial copy for Moki Cough Syrup. Off that one-minute audition, an inexperienced 18-year-old was hired: No. 1, because I convinced Breedy I could read; No.2, because I had an apparently pleasant voice; and No.3, because they were not required to pay me a lot of money—$14.20 a week, to be exact.

That's the way I started a career that eventually led to my induction into the Broadcasters' Wing at the National Baseball Hall of Fame in Cooperstown, New York, some 54 years later.

I've often thought, if Jean had not attended the dance that night and dared me, would I have wound up as a radio announcer? There's room for doubt.

But that was only the first of a series of accidental events of fate that led me first into radio and later, inexorably, into play-by-play broadcasting.

The second occurred in 1941 when Rose Heffner, a former high school classmate, and I decided to get married on November 15th, my only Saturday off during the football season.

But our plans were upset when about a week before the scheduled wedding, the folks at WEEU called and asked if I could fill in for announcer Dave Brandt, who was feeling ill and wouldn't be able to cover the Franklin and Marshall game on the 15th.

Rose and I felt, and our parents agreed, that we needed every dollar for our marriage. So we agreed that I should work for the extra pay and postpone the wedding until after the football season. But on the Thursday before the game, WEEU called back and said Brandt had recovered and I wouldn't be needed.

So the on-again, off-again ceremony was on again for November 15th. Three weeks and one day later, the Japanese attack

Ain't the Beer Cold!

on Pearl Harbor plunged the U.S. into World War II—but now, as a married man, I was classified 3A instead of 1A.

Once again, that indescribable thing called fate had intervened. If Brandt had not recovered, I would have been single on Pearl Harbor Day (December 7th) and most certainly would have been called up long before my actual 1943 induction. Who's to say what would have happened if that had been the scenario?

Another such event occurred in 1946, after I returned from combat duty in Europe and had resumed my career at WIBG in Philadelphia.

Late in the baseball season, I was sent to Shibe Park on Radio Appreciation Day to describe a ceremony between games of a doubleheader which honored broadcasters Byrum Saam and Claude Haring.

In those days, the ballpark elevator was hand-operated and required a key to be put into motion. But when Saam and Haring were ready to come back upstairs, the operator was nowhere to be found.

By the time I finished my scheduled bit, Whitey Lockman of the New York Giants was about to step into the batter's box to start the second game, and, with Saam and Haring still absent, I tried to describe the game—without a scorecard, lineup, or anything.

When the regular broadcasters got back to the booth it was the bottom of the first inning. Accompanying them was Les Quailey of the N.W. Ayer Advertising Agency, long one of my most ardent supporters, who suggested they work with me for a while.

With the broadcast veterans on either side of me, I was allowed to continue at the microphone for two innings. I loved it, and it was good for my confidence to be doing play-by-play on a 26-station network.

This impromptu audition led to me being added to the broadcast team in 1947 for the Phillies and A's home games. I've wondered many times over the years, what would have happened had the elevator man been on hand to bring Saam and Haring back on time. Would I have wound up in play-by-play? Would I have wound up in baseball?

4

Destiny, Fate, or Good Fortune?

Now let's fastforward (a word that didn't achieve popular usage until late in my career) to 1948, and the final episode in the quartet of events which helped shape my career and life.

That year I was sent to Baltimore to do color commentary for the Navy-Missouri football game on the Mutual Radio Network. Connie Desmond was to do the play-by-play.

The site for the Saturday game was then called Municipal Stadium. It had wooden seats and a sunken playing field, but what I remember most were those rats as big as cats that I saw running around when I visited the day before. Memorial Stadium was built on the site a few years later and it became my home-away-from-home for the next 30-plus years.

I expected to meet Desmond at a dinner Friday night, but he didn't show, and he was still among the missing on Saturday morning at the stadium.

Connie finally showed up about 20 minutes before airtime, did a little preparatory work, left again briefly and then came back just before the kickoff.

I did my opening, some seven or eight minutes of setting the scene for the intersectional rivalry, talking about the teams and the kind of offenses they ran, that kind of stuff, and turned the microphone over to Connie.

Was I in for a surprise! Connie thanked me, made some remarks, and then said, "Now for the play-by-play, here's Chuck Thompson." With that, he put on his hat and coat, and *walked out of the booth*—leaving me kind of unprepared, to say the least. Frankly, I was almost totally lost, without lineups, numerical charts or spotters' boards—and talking to listeners on more than 200 stations across the country.

Somehow, I staggered through it with the help of Les Quailey, who once had been a spotter and an assistant statistician for a guy whose name you may recall—Ted Husing, one of the all-time greats in sports broadcasting. In those days, Husing was to radio what Vin Scully is today, a gifted wordsmith and play-by-play announcer.

We found out later that Connie was a very sick man. He had

5

gone from the stadium directly to the railroad station and boarded a train for New York. On reaching the Big Apple, he was whisked from the train on a stretcher and taken straight to a hospital. He was confined for quite some time before he was able to return to work.

But Connie's misfortune provided a dramatic boost to my budding career. My appearance had been setup by the Gunther Brewing Co. and the Ruthrauff and Ryan Advertising Agency as an on-air audition while they sought to replace Baltimore legend Bill Dyer as the broadcaster for International League Orioles games.

The N.W. Ayer Agency had the baseball rights in Baltimore and, once again, Les Quailey was back in the picture. He recommended me for the job.

But if I hadn't replaced Desmond on the Mutual Radio Network, I might not have come to Baltimore, where it was my good fortune to be the right guy at the right place and time as the Colts and Orioles moved to the top of their respective sports.

Those strange twists that helped shape my career made me wonder whether destiny, or something, took a hand in leading me along the path that led to Cooperstown. Maybe this is what God intended for me to do. Call it destiny, fate, or good fortune, it certainly had as much to do with my career as any natural ability I might have had.

It didn't hurt a bit that God gave me a pretty good voice, but learning how to use it was another matter. I used to tell my father I looked as though I had "been put together with spare parts" and he always answered, "How about the pipes, kid!" Yes, the voice always had been there, even if at first I didn't know what to do with it.

Looking back, I just have to think I was a very lucky guy. I fell into something I could do without any previous training and then was befriended by a mix of people who saw something in me that could be honed with a little bit of encouragement and direction.

The two fellows who really worked on me were Les Quailey and Doug Arthur, the program director of radio station WIBG in Philadelphia. The two of them taught me and established me in

Destiny, Fate, or Good Fortune?

play-by-play, the basic fundamentals that kept me employed for all these years. I'm forever grateful to those two gentlemen.

Arthur used to talk with me every year about my future. In 1948, he said I had gone about as far as I was going to go in Philadelphia unless Saam moved to another city. Late in the year, I was doing Ivy League football when I was sent to Baltimore for that Navy-Missouri game.

I'm sure the decision to hire me to do International League baseball in Baltimore was partially, if not completely, due to what they heard on that on-air audition.

I don't know what I would have done, if not broadcasting. Once I started, I didn't want to do anything else, and play-by-play got me out of the studio. I was an average studio announcer. I could do record shows and liked modern music, and enjoyed that kind of duty. But, I had no training as a newscaster and, even with the voice, I was terrible on that assignment. I didn't have a feeling for news, like the late Galen Fromme had or Alan Walden has now on WBAL Radio in Baltimore.

I just happened to like sports, played some as a youngster, and was able to describe what I saw. If you are trained for this job, that's one thing. I had to learn my trade without formal training and to rely not on a placement office, but on chance and circumstance to clear a path. To think I started in the business in 1939, here it is1996 and I'm still talking into a microphone—seems like it must be a billion words by now. There were a million laughs along the way to go with all those words, and I've had many unforgettable experiences with show business and sports celebrities, and with the average Joe and Jane Fan who, in fact, made my job possible.

I had brief encounters chatting with Bob Hope and movie actress Sylvia Sydney; conducted a traffic-stopping interview with actor Edward Everett Horton; was a one-person audience for a live Bing Crosby performance on a transcontinental air flight; and had a flirtation with the lovely Grace Kelly (it was a flirtation for me; for Grace, it was just a nodding acquaintance) before she became a movie star and married Prince Rainier of Monaco.

Ain't the Beer Cold!

Along the way, I spent many an enjoyable night in the presence of Toots Shor, the *bon vivant* saloonkeeper who entertained many athletes and media members at his New York establishment.

The list of my friends in sports reads like a Hall of Fame, and for good reason: many have been inducted into the Halls of Fame of their respective sports.

They include Brooks and Frank Robinson, Jim Palmer, Robin Roberts, Earl Weaver, Boog Powell, Dave McNally, and Elrod Hendricks from baseball, and Johnny Unitas, Raymond Berry, Lenny Moore, Arthur Donovan, Gino Marchetti, and Jim Parker from football.

When I wrote my speech for the Hall-of-Fame induction, I got to thinking about the unseen audience of people who have accepted me in Baltimore for three or four generations. There's no way you can get into the Hall of Fame without their acceptance.

After my induction into the Broadcasters' Wing of the Baseball Hall of Fame, I received some memorable letters from listeners. I took 90-some on the first roadtrip the Orioles made in 1993, to Texas. I started to read some and only got through about four or five when I had to quit because they made me so emotional.

Last, but not least, my success is directly due to the years of selfless, unending support from my three children, daughters Sandy and Susan, and son Craig. It wasn't anything we ever mentioned, but there were some things that weren't obvious to the listening audience.

It's awfully hard to tell a six- or eight-year-old why their father has to leave on Christmas Day to broadcast a football game, why he wasn't home on Thanksgiving, or why they had to take a vacation on the beach at Ocean City without him (except for being able to hear him on the radio).

I now have seven grandchildren and in 1993 I became a great grandfather for the first time. That's a pretty good life, especially considering that I am healthy enough to enjoy it at the age of 75.

My wife, Rose, who died of cancer in 1985, did a remarkable job raising the kids. I guess I'm prejudiced, but it seemed to me

Destiny, Fate, or Good Fortune?

that, as I watched my children grow up, both Rose and the kids had to be Hall-of-Famers, too.

I married again in 1988 to Betty (Kaplan), a lady I had known casually for 10 to 15 years (and was then a widow), and she has provided my life with love and stability. Among the wonderful things she has done for me was to take me back to the church. Thanks to Betty, I joined church again, attend as regularly as I can, and do whatever I can to help the congregation. It's a little, old church, but it's my church and I like it very much.

In the original draft of my Cooperstown speech, I included just about all the names and events mentioned above. But I decided to cut it at the last minute. First, because the crowd was sitting in stifling heat and, second, because it was induction day for Reggie Jackson. That's why we go to Cooperstown every year, to honor an athlete being inducted into the Hall of Fame. The fact that they also honor a newspaper man and a broadcaster is just icing on the cake.

Although I made some hefty cuts in my speech, I also added one phrase at the start. For years in my game broadcasts I had used the expression, "Ain't the beer cold!" when things were going especially well for the home team. I got that phrase from Bob Robertson, a spotter who worked with me on Baltimore Colts football games (that were sponsored by the makers of National Beer).

Eventually, I received lots of mail from people in the Carolinas, the area sometimes referred to as the Bible Belt. The listeners felt they shouldn't have to put up with my ad libs about beer with all the beer advertisements they were already exposed to, and I thought they had a legitimate beef. So, I stopped using the line sometime in the 1970s.

I also discontinued another phrase I once used to celebrate something special on the field: "Go to war, Miss Agnes!" That was something I picked up from Bob Sharman, a golfing friend and neighbor. When his putting didn't improve after he read a book on the subject, Bob would grumble, "Go to war, Miss Agnes," after missing a putt.

I phased that expression out of my play-by-play lexicon as the

Ain't the Beer Cold!

Vietnam War dragged on. It was something I could no longer justify, because of the mounting American casualties.

But as I spread my notes on the dais, I was suddenly aware of my extreme good fortune and reacted the way I would have for a Frank Robinson grand slam home run or a John Unitas touchdown pass. So, I started my speech with a phrase out of the past, one that I could no longer resist:

"AIN'T THE BEER COLD!"

Chapter 2

Cooperstown: The Ultimate Prize

Betty and I were in our winter home near Bradenton, Florida, on February 9, 1993, when the telephone rang. She answered, handed it to me, and said, with a bit of a frown on her face, "It's something about the Hall of Fame."

"Do you know who's calling?"

"No."

"OK, fine. I'll take care of it."

The caller was Bill Guilfoile, vice president of the National Baseball Hall of Fame.

I said, "Hello, Bill, what can I do for you?"

As soon as he answered, I thought I detected a note of joy in his voice and he soon confirmed that perception. Bill said it was his pleasure to inform me that I was the 1993 winner of the Ford Frick Award, meaning I was going into the Broadcasters' Wing at the Hall of Fame!

While Bill continued to talk, I realized that for a long time I hadn't said a word. Finally, I remember asking if I had ever thanked him. Bill kind of laughed a little and I said, "Bill, I guess I'm not handling this very well. Have other nominees had any difficulty when you informed them?" I felt better when he said it was a normal reaction.

Ain't the Beer Cold!

Bill told me when the announcement would be released, adding that I should not divulge the information to anyone.

"How about my immediate family?"

"Of course, you can tell them."

When we ended the conversation, I told Betty, and we just kind of hung on to each other and cried a little bit because for a guy in my business this was the absolute ultimate recognition.

I had never really thought much about achieving this high honor. In past years, I was just happy for the guys who had been selected and felt they were deserving.

Honestly, I thought if I had a chance to be in a Hall of Fame it would be in the Football Hall of Fame in Canton, Ohio. Then I found out a couple of years ago that football doesn't honor broadcasters.

People would say over the years that I belonged in the Hall of Fame. It was well intentioned, but I felt they were just trying to be nice to me. I just never felt that I belonged. I'd look at the names—Mel Allen, Red Barber, Vin Scully, Ernie Harwell—and Chuck Thompson? Nah, that last name just didn't seem to fit.

As soon as I could, I called my three children to give them the news. I wouldn't say we cried, but it was pretty sentimental, very emotional.

One thing came to mind as I talked with my children: that making the Hall of Fame might help them understand all those celebrations I had missed at home, because I had to cover games around the country. That's just part of the price you have to pay if you're going to be in this business.

Soon after the official announcement was made a couple of days later, I started getting phone calls of congratulations. Ernie Harwell, my sidekick as an Orioles' broadcaster in 1955 and 1956 and who had already received the Ford Frick Award, was one of the first to call.

Bill White, president of the National League and himself a former broadcaster, was another caller. I also heard from Brooks Robinson, Jim Palmer, and Robin Roberts, all former Orioles who had been inducted into the Hall of Fame.

Cooperstown: The Ultimate Prize

I talked personally with Brooks and Jim, who called from a Bob Hope golf tournament in California. Both had said over the years that they thought I belonged in Cooperstown. Robin left a message on my answering machine saying how happy he was for me before adding: "Remember one thing, Kiddo, you'd have never made it if it hadn't been for those other guys. Who were those other guys?"

The next day I went to an Orioles' Dream Camp, where I was asked to introduce the old-timers on the field. I told the crowd about Robin's message and then proceeded to introduce some of those "other guys"—like Brooks Robinson, Boog Powell, and Mike Cuellar.

Before the day was over, a little lad approached with a felt pen and asked me to autograph a bat he was carrying. After I signed, he suggested I also put "HOF, 1993" under my signature.

I confess that I didn't know what he meant until the kid explained that HOF stood for "Hall of Fame." Until he pointed that out to me, it still hadn't been ingrained in my mind. But that simple request, and similar ones which followed, impressed upon me where I was headed.

The induction was not scheduled until August 1st, so there was no immediate rush to write my speech. First, I tried to answer all those who had sent congratulatory notes. I received some mail that was unbelievable. I could not fathom some of the things they had written about listening to me down through the years.

One guy apologized for writing a letter on a legal pad, but said he "felt it was much too important to put in a typewriter." Another said he started listening to me when he was 15, was now married with a son who is 15, and he still listens to me.

My family asked me to save some of the mail in an album, and I think I will. For all the years I've been in the business, I've never kept any mementoes or trophies. If you visit my home, you'd be hard-pressed to know what I did for a living.

But I will, of course, keep the framed certificate that I was presented by the Hall of Fame. And the mounted bat I received from Hillerich and Bradsby (makers of the Louisville Slugger)

13

Ain't the Beer Cold!

with Ted Williams' name on it, next to an engraved drawing of the Hall of Fame, will certainly find a place of honor in my home.

After being notified by Guilfoile, I had a lot of trouble telling people about my good fortune. But I had lots of time to contemplate how fate had led me down the road to Cooperstown.

I finally started writing my speech in July, in longhand on a legal pad, and made two or three drafts. I tried it out on Betty, my agent Ron Schapiro, and a longtime friend, Walter "Bud" Freeman, former promotions director of the Orioles. They all seemed to like it and that made me feel more at ease about what lay ahead.

Since Reggie Jackson was the featured honoree, I included what I considered an amusing anecdote from the slugger's one-year stay with the Orioles:

> We all know about his exploits on the field. I'd like to recount just one episode that I saw at Memorial Stadium involving Jim Palmer and Reggie Jackson.
>
> As you know, if you've seen Jim Palmer in action, he was one of the great traffic directors of all time. He kept moving outfielders (and) infielders, and he could do that because he was such a good pitcher, he knew he could get the ball where he wanted it to be, and the players respected him.
>
> He turned one day, I think we were playing the Minnesota Twins, and looked out to Reggie in right field and Reggie looked up. Palmer wagged the glove and Reggie took one step. Palmer stared at him and Reggie took a second step. Palmer continued to stare and Reggie took one more step.
>
> Palmer turned around and went up on the mound. Palmer worked on the batter who hit a flyball to right field. Reggie stood there and didn't have to move. He caught the ball and then, ladies and gentlemen, he took off his cap and bowed to Mr. Palmer.

I also told of Reggie hitting a batting practice pitch over the right-field wall at Oriole Park during the celebrities' home run contest the day before the All-Star Game earlier that year in Baltimore.

Reggie came to the plate at the urging of fans who chanted the familiar, "*Reg-gie, Reg-gie*." Then, after hitting the BP homer, he treated the fans to his home-run trot around the bases. That episode, I thought, was indicative of the great presence that Reggie exuded in uniform.

I included two of my favorite Casey Stengel stories that I was sure would be appreciated by the New York fans who came to Cooperstown to honor Reggie and who once cheered Hall-of-Famer Casey when he managed the Yankees.

One of the stories occurred during one of the American League Championship Series involving the Orioles and the Athletics during the 1970s:

> I happened to be in a restaurant in Jack London Square (in Oakland) called the Elegant Farmer, a wonderful restaurant. And that night, Mr. Finley (A's owner Charlie Finley) decided he would have a little fun and he brought his favorite mule, the one and only "Charlie O" down to Jack London Square, unloaded him—and walked him right into the Elegant Farmer.
>
> Right in front of that mule was a table full of executives from the American League and among those, Mr. Casey Stengel. Charlie walked the mule over, (and the mule) put his head down and kind of nuzzled Casey Stengel.
>
> Stengel looked up at that mule and said, "Mighty remarkable horse. He hasn't seen me for a year and he still remembers."

I also told another memorable Casey anecdote from the Yankees' spring training camp in St. Petersburg:

> We closed the tavern in the hotel that night and Casey

went to the elevator. The elevators were not operated by push buttons in those days, you had to have a guy cranking it to run it.

Casey walked in there and said to the guy running the elevator, "Here, I got to get some autographs on this ball and give it to a kid. If any of the guys come in, have them sign it for me, will you?"

Seven o'clock the next morning Casey was the first man in the dining room, here comes the elevator operator getting off duty, walked up to Mr. Stengel, handed him the baseball, said, "There it is, Casey." Stengel looked at it and there were were four signatures on it—and he fined each one 50 bucks for breaking curfew.

Because of my decision to trim the speech, I deleted stories about ponderous Boog Powell hitting an inside-the-park home run in Seattle and stealing seven bases in half a season after Earl Weaver took over as manager of the Orioles and gave Boog a cautious green light on the bases. Boog accented Weaver's approach to the game, stealing in his first game as manager; Boog had but four stolen bases in the six previous seasons.

I also cut out a story of how I choked up the day of the first landing on the moon when Fenway Park fans stood as one after the landing was reported by the public address announcer, applauded, and then sang, "God Bless America," after the song was started by one fan in the stands.

Also deleted was what I considered the single most effective and moving gesture I'd ever seen given by one player to another.

It happened on Brooks Robinson Day in Baltimore, when Brooks' successor at third base, Doug DeCinces, came out of the dugout to represent all the Orioles. He stopped momentarily at the spot Brooks once owned and yanked the bag from its mooring and presented it to the retiring Old Master—and didn't have to say a word. The crowd understood the significance, and responded accordingly.

As a result of my quick editing, I failed to thank Doug Arthur

Cooperstown: The Ultimate Prize

and Les Quailey and that really bothered me. I was also upset because I didn't get out to say hello to all those people who had made the trip from Baltimore.

But all the podium guests were sequestered in a high school gym before we went out to the stage together. I guess I could have sneaked out for a few minutes, but they told us not to leave the gym. I thought I'd better play by their rules, since they had been kind enough to invite me.

As I approached the microphone, I experienced some deliberately planned self-directed fear designed to force an attitude that would cause me to bear down. I felt that if I kept that cutting edge, I could maintain my professionalism and not break down in front of the crowd.

I'm not the kind of person who can turn it on and off. If I once broke down, I would find it very difficult to regain my composure.

I thought the people of Baltimore deserved better than that. I held up pretty well until I got near the end and then I bit down real hard and managed to finish:

> So I say to you that if sometime in the future you return to this wonderful town of Cooperstown and you go to the Baseball Hall of Fame Museum and you happen to go into the Broadcasters' Wing and a member of your group looks up at Chuck Thompson's name on that plaque and asks, "Did you know him?" I hope that you will say, "Yes, I did.
>
> "He was a friend."

Chapter 3

Growing Up in East Reading

I was born on June 10, 1921, long before the advent of television, and grew up when families more or less had to entertain themselves.

In that respect, the Thompsons did quite well. Ours was a house full of music, including a player piano, and Dad would break out in song whenever he got the urge. He also wrote poetry.

The player piano was in use mostly on weekends (maybe because Dad was traveling much of the time in midweek), pounding out such tunes as "Ramona," "Four-Leaf Clover," "Red River Valley," and a stirring march that was a family favorite, "Under the Double Eagle."

Dad was part of a trio that performed around town at church dinners and other functions. A neighbor, "Mac" McGregor, played the guitar, and Doug Lightbody was the other member of the trio of singers. Once Dad wrote lyrics to a song he called, "Old 97" which honored the memory of a friend, train engineer Jake Foss, who had died in a train wreck.

Dad was a performer almost until his death in 1988 at the age of 91, less than a month before he was scheduled to be the best man at my marriage to Betty. He passed away on September 1st and we were married on September 24th.

Growing Up in East Reading

I remember when I first introduced Betty to Dad, who was then blind. He extended his right hand but Betty, who never had to apologize to Jane Russell or Mae West or others similarly endowed, gently pushed the hand aside, stuck out her ample bosom, gave him a bear hug, and said, "In our family, we don't shake hands...we hug." Dad was obviously pleased.

They hit it off immediately and the next time I called Dad to tell him I was coming to see him, he asked, "Are you bringing Betty?"

While living in a West Reading nursing home, and blind for the last five or six years of his life, Dad would entertain the nursing home residents by singing and telling stories.

I guess you might say the ability to perform in public and the singing voice came down through my genes. So did my ample nose, which also was a hand-me-down from Dad.

I was born in Palmer, Massachusetts, and was christened Charles Lloyd Thompson as the first child of Lloyd Stevens Thompson and his wife, the former Maggie Moon. Sister Catherine was born some three years later. Dad, at 6-foot-1, towered over Mom's 4-foot-10 frame.

Dad was an outgoing guy, a perfect personality for a salesman, and enjoyed being around people. Mom was more low-key, and, despite her slight stature, she ruled the roost at our house until she passed away in 1972.

Dad had another son, Frank (about five years older than I, from a former marriage) and he joined our family when I was about 14 or 15. We were a middle-class family that had to struggle at times during the depression. But if we were economically depressed, as later sociological studies may have suggested, we were unaware of it growing up.

Sure, sometimes we wore cardboard in our shoes while we awaited needed repairs and Christmas gifts weren't extravagant, but we always had food on the table and there was love and happiness in our closely knit family.

As I recall, at the time of my birth, I think Dad was employed as a telegrapher, either for the Boston and Albany Railroad or the

Ain't the Beer Cold!

Central Vermont. Later, when we lived in Springfield, Massachusetts, or across the Agawam River in Feeding Hills, he was a uniformed police officer.

The family moved to Reading, Pennsylvania, just before I started first grade in 1927 after Uncle Charley Dowd arranged a job interview for Dad with the Hartford Steam Boiler Inspection and Insurance Co.

Dad was hired as an insurance salesman for Hartford and was assigned eastern Pennsylvania as his territory. But he remained fascinated with his old line of work and was still transporting prisoners at the age of 84 as an assistant deputy sheriff in Mount Penn.

One memory still lingers from the early years in Springfield, what you might call my introduction to radio at the age of three or four. At times I was left with a babysitter when Mom and Dad would go out for dinner, maybe once a month, the sitter would put earphones on my head and I would listen to KDKA in Pittsburgh. For me, that was fascinating.

Dad had a pet nickname for Mom, "Skooks," and I still don't know what it meant or its origin. Mom would use "Dear" or "Honey" when addressing Dad, but when she was displeased it would always be a much sterner "Lloyd." Mom always called me "Charles," while to everyone else, in and out of the family, I was "Chuck."

I was much closer to Dad than Mom, probably because we were able to talk sports and went hunting and fishing together. We used to kill squirrels when we hunted in Pennsylvania, but one year Mom developed a friendship with squirrels. They won her over by responding when she tapped on a metal railing of the front porch. After that, squirrels were no longer fair game in the Thompson household.

Squirrels may be merely rodents to most, but Mom, like many other observers, found them much more appealing because of their fluffy fur and cuddly appearance—or better packaging, as Madison Avenue might explain.

A couple of times a month, Dad would leave on Tuesday to

Growing Up in East Reading

cover his insurance route and return on Friday. But it was not traumatic since we kids expected it as part of the family routine.

Even after moving to Pennsylvania, I didn't lose my connection with Massachusetts. Starting at age nine or 10, my parents would drive me back to Palmer at the end of the school year to stay with Aunt Carrie, Dad's sister. My sister Catherine would go along for the ride, but she always returned with my parents.

All three would come back for two weeks later in the summer when Dad went on vacation.

The trip to Palmer would evolve into a 300-mile singalong, with Dad the resident choirmaster. Along the way, he would break into the Amherst College fight song whose lyrics honored a British general, Jeffrey Amherst, for whom the college was named. A couple lines of the lyrics went:

> *"Lord Jeffrey Amherst was a soldier of the king and he came from across the sea,*
> *To the Frenchmen and the Indians he didn't mean a thing in the wilds of this wild country."*

That was one of my favorite college songs as a kid.

We used to listen to Boston Red Sox radio broadcasts in Massachusetts. Grandmother Thompson, Dad's mother, was an ardent Sox fan who seldom missed a game on radio, a practice she continued almost to the end. She died a month short of her 100th birthday.

The highlight of my visits to Palmer, the biggest day of each summer, was when my cousins would take me to Boston for a doubleheader between the Sox and the New York Yankees.

It was an 86-mile trip down the Boston Post Road, since replaced by the Massachusetts Turnpike, to fabled Fenway Park. We knew we were there when we saw "Socony," the sign of the Flying Red Horse that we jokingly called "SOCK-ony" (in honor of the Sox). During the summer after my junior year of high school, I think it was, we saw Hall-of-Famer Lefty Gomez pitch for the Yanks.

Ain't the Beer Cold!

Dad said his mother once ran a boardinghouse in North Brookfield, Massachusetts, where former Philadelphia A's owner/manager Connie Mack lived as a young man when he worked in a shoe factory. Mack maintained the Brookfield connection when he took over the A's. He brought his team back to that area in the summer, perhaps on an off-day on the way to Boston for a series, to play a team of all-stars composed of players from the various milltowns.

My most vivid memory of the A's in those days was watching Indian Bob Johnson play left field. Every inning, it seemed, he took three or four baseballs with him to the outfield and tossed them to the fans before play resumed.

There were a lot of things to do in that small town to stay busy, including getting into mischief. I recall occasions when a bunch of us would go to a spring behind the high school, some 300 to 400 yards from any street, roll up some grape leaves in newspaper and do some smoking. We'd sit there fanning the smoke, afraid that it might be detected by a passer-by. How the times have changed!

One of the highlights of summer would be the day that Hatchey Hall's father, who worked on the Central Vermont railroad as a brakeman, would let some of us ride in the caboose on a roundtrip to Brattleboro, Vermont. What a treat!

When I got old enough, maybe 15 or so, I took a big step in my development when I started to work with cousin Fred on a milk truck. I regarded it as educational and informative, and besides, I got to stay up all night without sleep! That was really great, until I finally realized I couldn't go without sleep forever.

The milk truck was a four-cylinder International and when I said I wanted to drive, Fred gave me a challenge. He said if I could start the fully loaded truck on a 45-degree grade in Munson and not stall, I would be allowed to drive. It took me about a month before learning to handle the stick on that grade.

From that point on, we shared the driving on the route and saw many interesting sights in the early morning hours. We used to stop at Dunn's Diner and have breakfast at about 5:30 A.M. and a half hour later on Main Street, south of Palmer on the way to

22

Growing Up in East Reading

Munson, Fred would pull into a driveway at the end of the street and work on the bills for 10 to 15 minutes.

I used to think, why didn't he work on the bills when we were in the comfort of the diner? That puzzled me until one morning, as we were parked, I heard a female voice say, "Hello, Smitty," and Fred responded with, "Hey, how ya doing?"

I turned around to see a very attractive young lady and when she bent to pick up the milk, I realized why Fred parked in that driveway every morning—hoping against hope that the fair (and busty) maiden would appear to retrieve the milk.

Another less sensual treat would be hitchhiking to Forest Lake for an outing. Four or five of us would take to the road, toting our swim trunks, to bum a ride. In those more innocent days, no motorist would think of driving past hitchhikers if they could fit in the car.

During the summer in Palmer we played a great game at the end of Pleasant Street. We'd cut off a mop handle to make a simulated bat, and hit a pitched tennis ball while using a barn as the backstop. I held the record one summer with a hit that cleared *two* houses!

In Reading, I was more involved with organized sports, including sandlot baseball and high school football. Plus, there were a lot of pickup games on any open space whenever the guys got the urge.

The Reading area produced such baseball players as outfielder Carl Furillo of the Brooklyn and Los Angeles Dodgers and third baseman Whitey Kurowski of the St. Louis Cardinals, both of whom made multiple World Series appearances.

Also pitcher Randy Gumpert, who won 143 games for various Big League teams and Dom Dallessandro, a tiny 5-foot-6 outfielder who played briefly for the Red Sox but mostly for the Chicago Cubs.

I didn't spend much time thinking about my athletic ability because it was questionable at best. But I did have a love for all of the games.

I played some basketball at Southern Junior High School and

also tried soccer. But I wasn't so successful at soccer because it was a sport demanding speed, stamina, and agility—all of which I lacked.

An injury I suffered while playing junior varsity football at Reading High School upset Mom, and she put a temporary lid on participation in that sport.

A neighbor across the alley on South 16th Street, Dick Humbert, ran into a similar roadblock. His parents allowed him to play baseball and basketball, but not football. That was disturbing to all of us because we knew he was a better-than-average athlete.

The Humberts eventually moved to Richmond, Virginia, and before long Dick was playing football for the University of Richmond. It seems his parents merely wanted Dick to concentrate more on his studies in high school. They did allow him to play in college, and certainly didn't raise any objections when he signed with the Philadelphia Eagles and played as a wide receiver for a number of years in the National Football League.

Dave Abraham was another kid from the neighborhood who proved to be a late bloomer, for an entirely different reason. He was an outstanding center and linebacker but was stymied because he didn't like to study. As it turned out, however, he was a very bright man.

Dave went to Bullis Prep but quit the team because he didn't like the long walk between the playing field and the dressing room. But finally, he played at the Merchant Marine Academy, graduated as an ensign, and was on two ships that were torpedoed during World War II.

We had a lot of good people in the neighborhood around our house at 314 South 16th Street in Reading. (And since 1954, the same house number has been part of my life in Timonium, Maryland.)

Art Levan, who competed in the 1932 Olympics at Los Angeles, lived about four or five houses up the block from us. He was a weightlifter in the lightweight class, and qualified as our resident celebrity.

We lived in rowhouses separated by narrow alleys barely

Growing Up in East Reading

wide enough to walk through, similar to those in sections of Baltimore, with fenced-in backyards. You knew your neighbors, whether you wanted to or not. Perkiomen Avenue crossed 16th Street and was the main artery for trolley cars to downtown.

A playground at the grade school across the street was covered by macadam, and a wading pool about 18 inches at its deepest point, was added later. Young children, overseen by city employees, generally used the playground early in the day before teenagers moved in.

We had some dynamite volleyball games there, and after lights were mounted on surrounding buildings for security reasons, we had enough light for night games. We also played touch football, but the game sometimes evolved into tackling which played havoc with shoes and clothing.

That didn't go over well with all the mothers and fathers since money was not too easy to come by in those days. But I'd have to say we had good childhoods and never wanted for anything.

The greatest game we played in that area was known by the unofficial name of "Run Norman."

Norman Krause lived at the corner of 16th Street and Perkiomen Avenue. He was a couple years older than most of us, was employed and owned an automobile.

He hadn't participated in sports at school, but Norman could have been one of the great marathon runners of our time. He was the guy who, once or twice a month, we would chase all over East Reading.

It was an incredible way to spend an evening, chasing Norman down alleys and over fences. At 5-8 or 5-9 and about 140 pounds, he was extremely agile and could outrun all of us, whether we ran in a pack or separately.

Norman would leap over fences as if they weren't there and I don't know how he saw all the clotheslines. I know I didn't and sometimes I paid the price.

Never once did Norman say, "No" or "Knock it off." He loved the competition, simply because he never lost.

Eventually, we got smart and began chasing him in relays,

two or three at a time while the others rested. But that didn't work, either, until finally he would say, "OK, I've had enough fun," and let us close in on him.

We'd carry him back to the playground and drop him into the wading pool. He'd come up soaking wet, hollering and carrying on like a son-of-a-gun, and then start to laugh. And, that would be the end of the game.

A couple of weeks would go by and then all of a sudden someone would say, "Let's run Norman!" and the chase was on again. That was one of the great joys of growing up in East Reading. I often wonder what ever became of that likeable running fool.

When we weren't playing games, the guys just hung out. A favorite gathering place was called The Sugar Bowl, where we'd listen to jukebox music while snacking on sodas, cookies, and hot dogs.

I joined Joe Lombardo's band in 1938, my junior year of high school, and was paid $1 a night for singing eight to 10 songs, and a whopping $5 for a New Year's Eve gig. Mom got the money. The singing job continued when I started working and I also sang the lead in the class play.

After a couple of years away from football, due to Mom's concern over my jayvee injury, I made a comeback in my senior year after assistant football coach John Smith and Manny Jacobs, the physical education director, intervened.

They took me out of gym class one day and drove to my house for a conference with Mom, who was surprised by the unexpected visit. Smith and Jacobs assured Mom I would have the best of care and she finally gave her consent (Dad had already agreed). Later, Mom actually showed up to watch me play.

The season had already started by the time I joined the team and I lost some more playing time after suffering two shoulder separations.

A week after the first separation, we were due to play against Allentown, one of our chief rivals. Coach Hal Rock asked if I could play and, since the discomfort had eased, I said I thought I was ready. But in the first half, I suffered another shoulder

Growing Up in East Reading

separation and that was the end of my high school football career. I didn't know it at the time, but that was also the end of my baseball playing. The next spring when I tried to pitch, I seemed to be throwing well but the ball didn't go anywhere.

A star player for Bethlehem around that time was Chuck Bednarik, who went on to be one of the all-time greats in the National Football League.

Bednarik gave some idea about his versatility in high school. He played center, running back or fullback on offense, always played linebacker on defense, and also punted—and did the same in the NFL before being elected to the Football Hall of Fame.

In one game, coach Hal Rock complained about an official's call and came out on the field carrying the water bucket. As he put down the bucket and started yelling, he threw a sponge and hit the nearest person—who happened to be me.

"If you do that to me again," the coach shouted at the official, "I'm going to rip that shirt right off your back. Do you want that shirt ripped off your back?"

I played end and I was better on defense than on offense, in those days when you played both ways. I had good hands but absolutely no speed. The guy who played the other end, George Dracha, had such great hands he was able to catch the football one-handed like a baseball and he later played great basketball at Gettysburg College. When we ran downfield under a punt, George would yell, "Dah Gata Boom," in his best Pennsylvania Dutch, meaning the kick had been made and it was time to look up and locate the ball.

I scored just one touchdown that season, when an opposing back dropped the ball and old No. 47 (that's me) fell on it in the end zone.

After graduation, Coach Rock said I hadn't had a chance to display my talents in high school and suggested I come back to help him coach while also playing some sandlot football.

I heard that scouts from Lehigh were in attendance when I played my first game that fall for the East Ends against the Gaenzle Green Jackets. But I was thrown out of the game in the

27

second quarter for fighting with former teammate Dusty Rhodes.

That was embarrassing enough, but my parents were in the stands for the league opener, along with the mayor of Reading, and that made it worse. It was just one of those things that athletes do, like striking a match, and, bang, it's over that quickly.

When I came home, Mom said, "You ought to be ashamed of yourself." But she didn't have to admonish me...I *was* ashamed.

That was the start of my semi-pro career ($5 a game), and after my ejection I played six games and never sat down a minute. I played both offense and defense in the days before face masks and I had a helluva protuberance sticking out there between my eyes.

By that time, I had started working at WRAW Radio and every Monday I would show up at the studio with a skinned nose, a black eye, or puffed lips. The lip injuries were the worst because then I'd have a tendency to lisp or mumble while reading the copy on the air.

So I wasn't surprised when they gave me an ultimatum: either play football or be an announcer. I gave up an extra $5 a week, good money then, but I think I made the right decision when I quit football and concentrated on my first full-time job.

Chapter 4

The Start of My Career

It was the inimitable Ted Baxter, the inept anchorman on the "Mary Tyler Moore" show of the 1970s (and still in reruns), who frequently recounted how he began what only he considered an illustrious career. "It all started at a 5,000-watt radio station in Fresno, California," he would say in his best basso profundo voice.

Well, my own career in broadcasting had an even humbler beginning at WRAW, a 250-watt station in Reading, Pennsylvania. I started as a part-time replacement for employees on vacation and really knew very little about what I was trying to do.

But program director Paul Breedy turned me over to Cal Jackson, the chief announcer from the staff of WEEU, a sister-station of 1,000 watts, who explained the dos and don'ts of being a broadcaster. One thing he suggested was to try and read aloud as much as possible.

I'd sit at home and read the newspaper aloud, or go up to my room and read aloud from a book. But that didn't last long and I quit after four or five efforts.

I figured I could read reasonably well, but there is a difference between just reading and trying to sell through commercial copy. That's what they were trying to do, to get me to recognize the need to emphasize certain words.

Ain't the Beer Cold!

to this day when I sit for a recording session, it seems
e more "takes" I do, the better it sounds. But I didn't have
luxury at WRAW since all my commercials were done "live."

After a couple of days under Jackson, I'd sit with one of the
announcers and maybe handle a half hour program, introducing
records and reading commercials.

I learned how to record the time of a commercial on a log
sheet, as well as the time I gave the news, joined or departed the
network, or signed off. That part was easy but I had some problems with the various knobs and levers I encountered.

Engineers were in charge of the transmitters which relayed the
program to the airwaves, but the turntables and the control panel
or "board" were the responsibility of the announcers.

I have never had an aptitude for anything mechanical, which
I can best explain by recalling an anecdote from the 1970s. My
wife Rose and son Craig were in the den watching television,
probably in November, when Rose said, "Don't you think it's
time to take the air conditioner out of the window?"

"I'll do it now," I said, springing into action.

"Need any help, Dad?" asked Craig.

"No, I can take care of this. No problem."

I went upstairs and unplugged the air conditioner, then removed the screws which held it in place. So far, so good. But then
I made the mistake of opening the window and the device disappeared, falling into a tree alongside the garage.

The branch bent under the sudden weight and then
catapulted the air conditioner right through the garage window,
taking out both glass and frame. Fortunately, there was no car in
the garage.

When I came downstairs to get a broom, I could hear Rose
and Craig going absolutely hysterical. Feeling embarrassed and
more than a little stupid, I swept up the mess, then wrapped the
cable around the air conditioner and shoved it into a corner of the
garage, hopefully never to see it again.

But the next summer, Craig resurrected the air conditioner
and took it to his bedroom where it worked perfectly for another
two years.

The Start of My Career

With that kind of mechanical ability, WRAW was taking a chance with me in charge of the microphone, the turntables, and the access line to the (NBC) network.

There was a volume control on the microphone and each announcer had to be careful not to overmodulate, which would distort the sound. The dial didn't click, but there were markers on it from 1 to 10. After a few tests, you'd find the correct setting for your voice.

There was a turntable on each of the sides where the announcer sat like a secretary in front of a typewriter. They were used for records or commercial transcriptions and, by moving a switch, could be used at 33⅓ or 78 revolutions per minute.

The lower speed was for transcriptions and if you failed to move back to the 78 setting for a record, Bing Crosby might sound as though he were crooning in a vat of molasses. Conversely, if you failed to switch the other way, a commercial reading would resemble Mickey Mouse because of the high pitch and speed.

I encountered both problems several times, as well as making an introduction to the network only to encounter dead air when I forgot to throw the network dial or talking over someone when I joined the network too late.

But my biggest problem, and they told me it was a common error for beginning broadcasters, was failing to shut the microphone off when there was nothing official to say.

Several times following one of my mistakes with an open microphone, I used some expressions that may have been a fitting way to describe my stupidity but were certainly not fit for on-air consumption.

In the first week I made such unsavory remarks about three or four times and the last time, after I had rejoined the network, I told the engineer, "That's it, I just can't handle this. You can get somebody from WEEU to come over and finish the program." Then, I went home.

Fortunately for me, some understanding people from the station came out to our house and conferred with Mom, Dad, and me, and talked me into coming back. They said those things happen on occasion and that I should just go ahead and try to do better in the future. I went back.

I guess it might have been two weeks before I really relaxed and felt certain that the microphone was open and closed when it should have been, that the turntable speeds were set properly, and I was able to read commercials in an acceptable manner.

I was no longer terrified, but I did have more respect and understanding about what was expected of me. But over my long career, mistakes certainly were never completely eliminated. There were times that something slipped out that I wish I had never said.

After those traumatic experiences at the outset of my career, it was just a matter of going to work and doing something that I really enjoyed. Because I had played football, the station thought I'd be able to do play-by-play. I'd cover a high school or college game on Saturday and played sandlot football on Sunday until injuries affected my speech and I retired from competition.

In those days, the N.W. Ayer Advertising Agency out of Philadelphia controlled high school and college broadcasts on the Eastern Seaboard, from New England into the South.

Les Quailey, who was in charge of the announcers, came to hear me one day from outside the booth (there was not enough room for him inside) and he later taught me the fundamentals of football broadcasting.

At the time, I also learned from three extremely talented broadcasters who later, like I, ended up at WBAL Radio in Baltimore—Bailey Goss, Galen Fromme, and Melvin Quinn. Another alumnus was Charley Klemmick, known professionally as Charles Stark, who later went to CBS in New York.

When I had been at WRAW a couple of months, I was dispatched to do a remote, a broadcast that did not originate in the studio but from an on-site location. Remotes are fun to do because they get you out of the studio and are a definite change of pace.

My first assignment of that nature took me to the Rajah (pronounced in Reading as "rye-ah") Temple Theater on 6th Street to cover an American Legion convention.

The station was to broadcast the opening ceremony, and I was

The Start of My Career

sent to put it on the air and to sign off at the end. It seemed a simple enough duty.

I wrote out a sign-on of about a half-minute, making sure I had the commander's name correct and how it was pronounced, how the convention brought X-number of people to town, and how proud Reading was to host the meeting for the first time.

"To get the ceremony started," I said after being alerted by the engineer that we were on the air, "it is with a great deal of pleasure that I take you to the stage of the Rajah Temple Theater and commander...."

The commander acknowledged my introduction and made a few opening remarks as I sat down, relieved in the belief that my job was done until the sign-off.

But the commander then threw me an unexpected curve, better still, a knuckleball. After introducing some people, the stage was cleared and the audience watched a pantomime on the military, particularly about burials.

There was not a sound from the stage and, consequently, not a sound going out over the station until I came to my senses and tried to describe the pantomime. I did to the best of my ability, but it was the longest five minutes of my young life.

That was one of the most terrifying, panicky situations I had ever experienced, since they hadn't warned me in advance that it was coming. The speeches that followed were a piece of cake for the rookie to handle.

As a newcomer to the staff it was also my job on Sunday evenings to go to an assigned church and broadcast the evening service. Other men on the staff were married and had Sundays off. But I didn't mind doing the remote. After all, I was in radio, man, a real broadcaster!

Besides, it was a rather easy assignment. Acting as my own engineer, I checked to make sure the microphones and lines that had been installed previously were still working.

After informing the listeners of the name and location of the church, I'd introduce the pastor from a room just off the altar area and motion to the minister that he was "on," and then sat there until my sign-off.

Ain't the Beer Cold!

All I had to do was to watch an indicator needle to make sure the line was open and was not in the overmodulating position.

After doing a couple of church broadcasts, I realized that being an unattached young man, I might make good use of the time by inviting a young lady to watch a broadcaster in action and "help" me with the remote.

So I took a date one night, introduced her to the pastor, and then we both retired to the room for some get-to-know-each-other quality time before going out for a post-sermon Coke or sundae.

The plan sounded good on paper, giving me an hour or so to spellbind the young lady, but it wasn't as productive as I had hoped. First, we had to speak in whispers so the minister or congregation couldn't hear us.

In addition, I was then enough of a professional to be conscious of my prime job—to keep an eye on the needle to make certain it kept moving to indicate that WRAW listeners were getting the program.

That didn't prove too exciting to the young lady I had invited. I found out a couple of days later that she had talked to some of her schoolmates and told them all I wanted to do was watch that blasted needle. In other words, for her it was a very boring evening. So much for Thompson's attempts at spellbinding! From that point on, I had to do my needle watching solo.

One of the part-owners of WRAW and its chief engineer was Mr. Landis. I don't think I ever knew his first name but everyone called him Eggy, probably because of his bald head.

Eggy was about 5-foot-10, had a little wax mustache, always wore a beret, and definitely marched to a different drummer. He was very intelligent, probably borderline genius, when it came to electronics. But as for his presence around the station, Eggy was simply out of touch with reality.

He once came into the studio while someone was in the middle of reading a commercial, unlocked a ladder, climbed up, and hammered into place a sign that said, "Silence." Eggy was the first of the engineering breed I met down through the years and I found them to be in a world of their own.

The Start of My Career

Everywhere he went in the remote truck, Eggy took his pet poodle along for the ride. That meant if you were assigned to do a show and Eggy was the engineer, you had a poodle licking your ears and the back of your neck to and from the job.

Eggy went with me when I had my first big break at WRAW, broadcasting the Albright vs. Carnegie Tech football game at Albright Stadium in Reading. We were feeding the game back to Pittsburgh, where Carnegie Tech is located, so I was on a network—plus being paid a handsome extra $5!

I was as nervous as I could be, scared silly as I sat in the booth going over the names and numbers of the players, while Eggy climbed all over the place making connections. Finally, he came in and sat down, rubbed his hands in glee, and said simply, "OK, kid, let's go."

By that time I was getting pumped up for my debut, but even I knew something was missing and I asked Eggy, "Where are the microphones?" After a long pause, Eggy cursed and headed for the remote truck.

As an engineer he thought the most important thing was to get the line ready, and establishing the connection between Reading and Pittsburgh. He didn't think the microphones were quite that important.

Another job I inherited as a rookie broadcaster was to do a remote of the Easter sunrise service from Mount Penn in 1940.

Reading has a pagoda on top of Mount Penn and every Easter an electrically lighted cross is erected that can be seen for miles. The team for the broadcast included program director Paul Breedy, the guy who hired me and who came along for moral support, engineer Eggy Landis, and rookie Thompson. And, oh yes, Eggy's neck-licking poodle.

All I had to do was get the minister's name correct, the location and the name of the choir. While chairs for the choir and congregation were being put into place, Eggy was walking back and forth, stroking his mustache and apparently aggitated.

Finally, I hear him say, "Hey, Rev, come here a minute."

"What can I do for you?"

Ain't the Beer Cold!

"We've got a problem."

"What might that be?"

"See that cross (at 20 feet high and supported by guy wires, how could he miss it?)? I've got to put my equipment over there."

"What?"

"You're going to have to move that cross—that's where I want to put my equipment."

The voices raised a little bit, but Eggy was adamant. Breedy moved to intervene, trying to avoid an unpleasant experience.

The confrontation included a succinct summation from Eggy: "Rev, the Good Lord can see that damned thing just as well over here as he can over there. Now, get it the hell out of there."

But the minister held his ground, the cross stayed in place, and the Easter message followed. Amen.

Another character at WRAW was Lew Rogers, a former outstanding broadcaster on the Yankee Network in New England. He was kind of like Bailey Goss, big and good looking, with an outgoing personality and a great voice.

Unfortunately, he had a craving for "Red Eye." Every pay day he'd purchase a bottle, bring it back to the station in a brown paper bag and hide it in a men's room wastebasket. I first thought he had a kidney problem; I soon learned better.

When I first started at WRAW, I'd get a call to come to the station and replace Lew, but the program director never told me why. But it didn't take long before I found out, and learned of the men's room hideaway.

If Lew imbibed while working at night, when he was on the network and only had to read a few commercials and do an occasional station break, the only other person on duty was the engineer.

Lew would soon grow tired of the music being sent over the line from NBC. He'd disconnect the network, open the mike, and say, "Your announcer doesn't approve of that kind of programming. I think it's a waste of time and I'd like to have you listen to some of the world's most beautiful music."

Then he would play the same song, "Thine Alone," over and

The Start of My Career

over. WRAW was the most important thing in my life at the time, so I listened to it almost every minute of the day. Whenever I heard that familiar tune repeated, nobody had to call. I knew it was time to head for the studio as a relief announcer.

I tried to help Lew a little bit because he was a fine fellow (probably in his 50s, but to me that was old) who just needed some help to combat his problem. He returned my expression of concern a couple of years later.

Sober, Lew was one fine broadcaster. But he was given to exhibitionism which also got him into trouble and caused me some embarrassment.

Lew put a lady on the air one day to make a speech. She was a very pleasant person who stood about five feet tall and weighed in excess of 200 pounds.

I was watching from the control room, looking into the studio as Ms. Wide Beam read her copy and there was Lew behind her, doing a bump-and-grind routine. It was time to move quickly before Lew got us all in trouble.

I went outside and cornered him in the air lock outside the studio and told him, "Hey, her husband's outside and he might see you!"

When the speech was finished, Lew must have adjusted every microphone and chair in the studio, moved the piano and even straightened the rug, anything to stall for time. Sure enough, when he came out after some 15 minutes, the couple was gone. I don't think the husband saw anything.

WEEU, our sister station, put on a lot of country music bands. All sold some kind of product designed to make you feel better and all had ranches around Reading where they put on country music weekends.

One group called itself "Sons of the Pioneers," although it was not the one later connected with Roy Rogers, and one of the members was Eddie Cameron who later became Captain Video on television.

That group knew I sang in a dance band and was knowledgeable about music, so one day they asked me to critique a song

37

they had come across. They thought it was one of the great country songs of all time.

It didn't excite me and they played it again with the same result—the song did nothing for me. "If you guys like it," I said, "I hope you do well with it."

"We can't believe you don't like it," a member of the band countered.

"I didn't say that, I just don't think it will be a hit."

Well, what did I know? The song became very popular—and was called, "Deep in the Heart of Texas."

I was aware, however, that there was something more than just being a studio announcer and that thought kept bugging me. Although I liked playing the kind of music I enjoyed, I was unhappy that I wasn't able to get into sports.

In 1941, my girlfriend Rose and I contemplated marriage, and talked it over with our parents. It was just a matter of when.

That was when we set the date, talked about postponing it because of announcer Dave Brandt's illness, and then went through with the ceremony after Brandt recovered and I wasn't needed to broadcast the Franklin and Marshall game.

For our honeymoon, we traveled *all the way* to Philadelphia and as a newly married man I didn't have to go into the Army for almost two more years.

We moved to a new part of town after the wedding and were faced with a new problem: getting to work on time. WRAW was located at 6th and Penn Streets and the Reading Railroad line was on 7th Street.

About 7 A.M. every day, a passenger train stopped at the railroad station and the cars blocked my route to the studio. If I beat the train, I would be on time to put the station on the air at 7 o'clock.

But as a newlywed, I found it difficult to get out of bed in the morning and if I were held up by the train, the WRAW engineer merely played the National Anthem, over and over if necessary, until I arrived.

After I turned 21 in 1942, I was old enough to have a brew

The Start of My Career

legally and was then eligible to take the Penn Street challenge. Reading was a good old-fashioned Berks County Dutch-German community where beer drinking was an accepted mode of entertainment. My father made his own home brew and Mom assisted in the process, and I'm sure a lot of other families did the same.

The young guys in town would try to go down Penn Street, from 11th down to Front, then cross over and come back up, and see if they could have one drink in every bar. The challenge was to see how many establishments you could visit before you needed assistance.

Well, just before Christmas in 1941 (when I was still shy of turning 21), my old football buddy, David Abraham, and I tried the challenge. By the time we were on the second leg of the trip, we were getting a bit tizzy.

Along the way we came across a beautiful little Christmas tree, which we unplugged and took with us. When we reached the square which extended from 4th to 6th Street, we took the tree into the Crystal Restaurant which was on the ground floor beneath WEEU. The owner was Mr. Mandis, who had a son six to eight years older than the wandering duo.

When we plugged the tree in, it didn't light. Dave and I, definitely feeling no pain, were heartbroken and completely overwhelmed, and tears streaked down our faces. The tree wouldn't light, our evening had been crushed!

Mr. Mandis sized up the situation and poured us some coffee, and then more coffee—enough until we finally knew who and where we were. Then he said something I'll never forget:

"If you two guys ever want to try this again, I'll even pay the expenses—if you guarantee to start on my side of the street."

Early in 1942, as a married man I became much more aware of finances and the fact I had to pay for food and rent. Before, I never paid any rent at home and food was always on the table, and was able to do what I wanted with my salary.

At the time of our marriage, I was making $27.50 a week, plus another $5 talent fee for covering football. Fortunately, I married a *wealthy* woman who was making the princely sum of $60 weekly as a clerk-typist with Jacobs Aircraft in Pottstown.

Ain't the Beer Cold!

So finances were definitely on my mind when my tour of duty at WRAW ended abruptly early in 1942 after I did a show called "The Packard Dinner Bell," which was sponsored by the Packard dealer in Reading and was on both WRAW and WEEU.

The announcer who did the show on WEEU got a $2.50 talent fee, but I didn't get a cent when I did it on WRAW. I was upset and went in to see program director Paul Breedy.

He explained that sponsors pay more for commercials on the more powerful WEEU than they did on WRAW. I argued that shouldn't have anything to do with it; I should get the same fee, which represented nine percent of my weekly salary. Breedy disagreed, said he couldn't do anything about it, and suggested we go talk with the owner.

We did just that, and the argument started anew. I just felt I was being cheated and that was that. It became pretty heated and the next thing I knew, I couldn't see straight. I told him what he could do with his radio station and even volunteered to offer help if he needed it.

Just like that, I'm fired—I'm gone from the only two stations in Reading with no plans on what I would do next.

Chapter 5

Before I Was Rudely Interrupted

As it turned out, my unemployment didn't last long and I soon decided that I had made a significant career advancement because of my battle over a $2.50 talent fee.

The day after leaving WRAW, Cal Jackson phoned and suggested I contact Tommy Thompson, a former time salesman at WEEU who was then working at WKBN in Youngstown, Ohio.

Tommy told me he felt certain that I'd be hired at WKBN, but saw no harm in first stopping at WPIC in Sharon, Pennsylvania, close to the Ohio border, where he had promised to bring me in for an audition.

About four or five days after being fired, I passed the WPIC (whose slogan was "The Pick of the Dial") test and was told they would match any offer from elsewhere. But Tommy, who was doing the driving, wanted to complete our appointed rounds, so we continued on to WKBN.

Today, you don't have to audition in person; you just send in a tape and if they like the sound, you're called in for an interview. But in those days, you had to perform. At WKBN, I talked a little bit about myself, answered a few questions, talked about sports, and read some commercial copy and some news.

Ain't the Beer Cold!

Then Gene Trace, the program director, said, "Thompson, just ad-lib a little, tell us what the studio looks like." Well, it was a beautiful place, nothing like WRAW, and I had no trouble launching into a description. I wasn't keeping track of the time, but before long I had described the microphones, the color of the floor, the width of the room, the location of the lights, and even the Associated Press machines in the adjacent room.

Finally, by the time I had started to count the holes in the acoustic tiling, I thought, "I wonder if he wants me to continue?" Suddenly, the door opened and there was Mr. Trace.

"Thompson, I owe you an an apology," he said. "It's unforgiveable. I never should have let you run on like that, but I was so impressed that I went back to get the owner to ask him to come out and listen. I waited while he finished a phone call, and left you hung out to dry."

I was also impressed—by the great looking facility and WKBN being known as the "Voice of the Mahoning Valley." Besides, they held out a strong possibility I would eventually cover Ohio State football. That's all I had to hear...WKBN was for me.

Rose later came out to join me and we looked for an apartment. We had just vacated a beautiful apartment in Reading, in a mansion that had once been the private home of a former Pennsylvania governor and was later converted into apartments. It was somewhat plush for two young newlyweds (WRAW is now located in that building).

In those days, the technology needed to clean steel towns was not yet available, so Youngstown was, to put in bluntly, a dirty city. When I went to work on a trolley car downtown, I carried a clean shirt in a paper bag. When I arrived at the studio, I would remove the shirt I had worn on the trolley, which was already dirty, and replace it with the fresh one, and when I went home I would switch to the dirty one.

We lived in a ground floor apartment that was not very attractive. But we were young and in love, so what difference did that make? It was our first time out of Reading and since we didn't know anyone in Youngstown, we tried to be somewhat creative in finding things to do.

Before I Was Rudely Interrupted

As a result, Rose would ride the trolley with me to the studio and spend the evening with me as I read the news and sports copy.

While I did the 11 o'clock news, Rose would be listening on the headset as CBS informed those on the network which orchestra would be playing at the conclusion of the time set aside for the local news broadcast.

She would write me a note, like "Glenn Miller from the Paladium, playing 'Deep Purple.'" Then she'd place the headset on me so I could talk my way out of the newscast into the remote and introduce the band.

That's the way we spent our nights in Youngstown!

One night, about two weeks after joining WKBN, the phone rang in the studio and on the other end was a man who was to become vital to my broadcasting career—Doug Arthur, the program director of WIBG in Philadelphia.

He informed me that there was a job available if I were interested, at their studio in Glenside, a suburb of Philadelphia.

I asked Doug to hold a minute while I told Rose the news.

"I don't know whether I should take it," I said, and Rose responded quickly, succinctly, and clearly:

"If you don't take it, I'm on the next train home."

I then told Doug I would have to give two weeks' notice and then we'd be on the way. It was a good feeling to know that another radio station would think enough of me to call long distance to Ohio and offer a job in a bigger market and at a much higher salary, though I no longer remember the figure.

We were two happy kids that night. Including the two-weeks' notice, we were in Youngstown for only a month. I felt bad about leaving Gene Trace because he had been so good to us, but I knew I had to get somewhere closer to home and Glenside was only 56 miles from Reading.

We traveled to Reading by train, a mode of travel I've always enjoyed. I've had some wonderful times riding trains all over this country.

But in those days the trains were dirty, at least the one we took out of Youngstown fit that description. The windows rattled and soot from the engine and dirt from along the track seeped into the car. We sat up all night, and feeling dirty and uncomfortable didn't bother us a bit. We were going home and I had taken an important step in what was to be a long, long career.

I had been recommended for the job by Lew Rogers, the old pro from WRAW whom I had befriended when he had his battles with "John Barleycorn." He mentioned my name to Doug Arthur, so I'm indebted to him for recommending me and for teaching me a lot about commercial radio. When he was away from the bottle, Lew was as good as you needed to be. By then he had better control over his drinking problem, but he didn't last long at WIBG.

I didn't have to audition or read anything. Doug just wanted to talk with me for a time in general terms, about sports and news, while he was choosing records for his show. He just wanted to hear my voice and was concerned whether I knew anything about grammar. Finally, he said, "Just one more question. Who's your favorite band?"

At the time, Guy Lombardo was one of the most popular dance bands in the world, I guess, but my personal preference didn't run that way. And I thought if Doug were going to hire me, I had to be honest with him.

So I told the truth and answered, "Right now, at this moment, I think my No. 1 band would be Jimmy Lunceford." He had one of the great bands of modern jazz and as a 12-year-old, I went to one of his shows at the Astor Theatre in Reading. The ushers let me stay for three performances before they threw me out.

Doug smiled at my answer and said, "Kid, you're going to be OK."

Later, when I got to know Doug better, I reminded him of our conversation and asked if I would have gotten the job if I had named Guy Lombardo. He said, "You know, I would have had to think about that a little bit."

Actually, listeners to WIBG rarely heard any Lombardo tunes. They were more likely to hear bands like Benny Goodman, Glenn Miller, Harry James and the Dorseys, Jimmy and Tommy, and singers such as Frank Sinatra and Ella Fitzgerald.

Before I Was Rudely Interrupted

Doug thought that the announcers did their best work standing up, even for a 15-minute newscast...a time period that provided lots of opportunity to make life uncomfortable for the man in front of the microphone.

One of the running gags in the broadcast business is to make the announcer "break up" on the air, make him lose his concentration. Sometimes we'd wait until the announcer was in the middle of a 15-minute newscast, then start a fire in a wastebasket containing paper from discarded scripts.

But that might not be distracting enough. If not, the can and its burning contents would be pushed under the backside of the guy at the mike. He'd get uncomfortable and try to kick the can back, only to have it reappear again.

After that scene was repeated several times, the harried victim would run a forefinger across his throat to indicate he wanted the power turned off by the engineer in the next booth.

But the engineer, while looking directly at the announcer, would ignore the "cut" sign. If the fire threatened to do more harm than intended, the perpetrator would be forced to end his practical joke by either dousing the flames or moving the basket out of harm's way.

The biggest change for me at WIBG was the jurisdiction of the engineer. The announcer still operated the turntables, but volume control was the engineer's responsibility. From his booth, the engineer was responsible for keeping track of that blasted needle that gave me so much trouble at the WRAW remotes.

All the announcer had to do was stand and introduce the music he was playing or read the commercials. The engineer took care of everything else.

In the early days of radio, each station had a house band. WIBG had a bunch of good Philadelphia musicians, but hardly as proficient as the Jan Savitt band which played at nearby WCAU.

Anyway, I was assigned to be the announcer for a show featuring our band. I was confident now, a pro, and I was in the big leagues.

I walked into the studio while the band was tuning up and I

looked at the copy set in front of me. I was thinking about the songs they were going to play and what I was supposed to do.

Everything was apparently fine, but somehow the microphone didn't seem to be quite right. So I reached up and loosened the screw holding the microphone in place so I could lower it a bit.

BAAAAD decision!

As I made the adjustment, engineer Paul Krantz burst out of the booth and laid me out verbally. Paul said if I were ever going to find another job in Philadelphia, I'd better learn to keep my hands off the microphone.

All the announcer had to do was to breathe and talk; the engineers got everything on the air. Despite that outburst, the engineers were absolutely great, and I remember them fondly.

Doug Arthur did the "Danceland" show twice a day, from 10:30 A.M. until noon and from 6 P.M. until 7:30, and it was the top-rated show in Philadelphia.

When he was free in the afternoon, Doug would get two tape recorders and take them and me to a high school basketball game to practice play-by-play broadcasting.

Nowadays tape recorders are compact enough to carry in your shirt pocket, but back then we had to tote around two bundles about the size of small suitcases. One was needed to provide and control power, the other to house the reels of tape.

We weren't broadcasting, just recording. I'd do two or three minutes of play-by-play, then stop and replay the tape for Doug to critique. He gave me valuable lessons that have stayed with me all my life.

At one of those sessions, I witnessed Wilt Chamberlain in a high school game. I only saw part of the game, but a brief look was all I needed to know that Wilt was something special.

Doug told me never to say an individual rebounds; instead give the name of the team, then mention the individual. He also suggested telling in which direction the team with the ball was moving, right to left or left to right.

Of all sports, I've found basketball the easiest to do, because there are only 10 players on the floor and the ball is big enough that you can't be fooled.

Before I Was Rudely Interrupted

Hockey was the most difficult for me to describe because there is no continuity of puck possession or direction. What you don't say is sometimes more important than trying to jam a thousand words into a short time span. Jim West, who covered hockey in Baltimore and later broadcast Chicago Black Hawks games, was a true master in describing the sport.

We also did tapes at football games and Les Quailey taught me the ABCs of play-by-play in that sport. He stressed giving the down, yardage, and team possession before each play ("Third down, six to go for the Colts on the Bears 27"). The announcer should never assume that the listener was paying enough attention to keep a running chart.

We made our own charts to keep track of the plays and penalties, because at the end of the game we might have to fill many minutes recapping the highlights.

In later years, when I did National Football League games for local broadcasts, or for NBC or CBS, I still used that system. Some announcers don't have to keep such extensive notes because they have better memories. But I've walked out of many football and baseball games when I've had to stop and think if someone merely asked the score of the game I had just described.

Les and Doug also tutored me on baseball play-by-play, as did Byrum Saam and Claude Haring during my first two years doing major league games.

They all said it was paramount in baseball broadcasts to say whether the pitcher was a righthander or lefthander and whether the batter hit from the right or left side, how the fielders were positioned, and whether the infielders were drawn in or playing in their normal locations.

Following the same principles as with basketball, every ball was hit to a position, not a player ("Mattingly hits a grounder to short, it's fielded by Cal Ripken...").

Some of those guidelines might be a bit less important now with the massive television coverage, but they still apply to radio broadcasts.

Those were the fundamentals, the basic principles of radio

play-by-play broadcasting, that those four men got through to me and made me understand. If you don't have that platform, you're not going to be successful. I truly believe their constant pounding paid off for me.

Everybody who ever listened to a baseball broadcast will always have the same complaint and 95 percent of the time the complaints are justified. Because people tune in and out, they say they don't hear the score enough. You simply can't give the score too often. That's why the late Red Barber had an egg-timer in the booth, to remind him that he should give the score at least every three minutes.

Jon Miller, the respected Orioles and ESPN broadcaster, still uses the egg-timer today and it's a good idea. It isn't written that a guy who turns on the game is going to stay with you every pitch. He may leave to do something else, but the minute he dials your way again, he would like to know the score, and he might even like to be reminded who's playing.

For the most part, I was a staff announcer to WIBG and did sports programs twice a day. I also gave the call letters during station breaks.

I slowly worked my way into doing play-by-play on college football for the N.W. Ayer Advertising Agency and their client, the Atlantic Refining Co., which sponsored college and high school football broadcasts along the Atlantic Seaboard.

I did Temple football on Friday or Saturday night. I also broadcast an occasional Ivy League game, like Princeton, Harvard, or Dartmouth, or did the color for Penn games with Byrum Saam on the play-by-play. All those jobs were sent my way by Les Quailey and I was paid a *$25 talent fee*.

WIBG was owned by John B. Kelly, a wealthy Philadelphian who started as a bricklayer and wound up owning the company. He was an Olympic single-scull champion and so was his son Jack (John, Jr.). There were also two daughters, one the lovely Grace who later became a movie star and a real-life princess.

Someone started checking one day and found that not one of the announcers at the station had a son. Then the survey began in

Before I Was Rudely Interrupted

earnest, and we soon realized there were also no sons among the salesmen, secretaries, or copywriters. It was natural, then, that WIBG became to stand for "Where Intercourse Begets Girls." So I guess it was only to be expected that our first child, born just after I returned home from Army service overseas, was also a girl.

Sometime late in 1942, we moved into new studios on Walnut Street, between Broad and 15th, in downtown Philadelphia, across from the Bellevue Stratford Hotel. After that move, I was in hog heaven. We had big, beautiful studios, a lot of wonderful people and great ratings. It was a perfect place for me because not only did they play the music I grew up with and loved, but they were also crazy about sports.

But hovering over my budding career was the war and my impending induction. So I decided to take matters into my own hands and take an exam to enter the Marines.

When I took the eye exam, however, I had difficulty reading figures that were hidden among the colored dots. Although I could point to various colors in the room, I couldn't decifer the dots and was told to come back in a couple of weeks for a retest.

I returned but the result was the same and that made me feel deficient and a little angry. Apparently, I couldn't distinguish between green and gray, a problem that made no difference when I was inducted into the Army on October 5, 1943.

While the world awaited an Allied invasion of Europe and to see what would happen to Adolph Hitler, I was wondering when, where, and if, I would ever resume my career.

Chapter 6

Just Call Me Sergeant

I traveled only a short distance to Indiantown Gap, Pennsylvania, to be outfitted for my uniform and receive my induction orientation. I looked around the room to see if I could spot any friendly faces and there was only one, Kenny Sensenig, who lived down the street from our house.

After a couple of days, some of us boarded a train for a new assignment without being told where we were headed. I was lying in a berth when we made a stop and I peaked out of the drawn shades and saw a sign which read, "Baltimore."

I didn't know anything about Baltimore then, but the city was to play a very important part in my life in the years to come. Our final destination was Camp Blanding, Florida, not far from Jacksonville, where I was trained to be a rifleman, first class.

After completing a 17-week infantry basic training course, I was offered a chance to qualify for Officers Candidate School. But the sergeants of B Company, 224th Infantry, all seasoned veterans, explained to me that I wasn't obligated to attend OCS; that I couldn't be forced to qualify. They further explained that the life expectancy of a low-ranked infantry officer in combat was something under five minutes. Hearing that, I decided I was definitely *not* OCS material.

Just Call Me Sergeant

I was held over for another cycle, only this time I would help with the training after being promoted to the rank of sergeant.

Some of the new trainees were in their mid-30s and not in the best of condition, unable to walk 18 miles carrying an 80-pound pack. I explained to the trainees to do the best they could physically and we'd teach them how to shoot the rifle and the rest.

A few guys were unable to keep up with the majority of the troops on hikes. One, about 32 years old, 6 feet and 250 or so pounds, was not accustomed to physical labor. When we went on a forced march, whereby the troops had to alternate running and walking for 10-minute stretches, I told him not to worry if he couldn't keep up, to walk a little longer if necessary.

While he was walking, the commanding officer, a first lieutenant, drove up from behind, jumped out of his jeep, hit the private in the back and pushed him into a ditch, putting him even further behind the platoon.

After hearing what happened after we returned from the hike, I confronted the lieutenant, yelling in a voice that could be heard throughout the company area. He soon became more than a little perturbed.

I was on the verge of punctuating my argument with fisticuffs when I was constrained by a Master Sgt. Jenkins, a strapping 6-foot-4, 225-pounder, who handled me with one arm.

The quick action by Jenkins (who was, incidentally, from Baltimore) saved me from being severely disciplined, but the outburst did end my stay at Camp Blanding. I was punished by being sent to Camp Howze, Texas, to be *retrained* in infantry basic.

That assignment turned out a lot better than I expected after a chat with my new commander, a Captain Green, whose nickname was "Hardrock." He asked if he were going to have any trouble with me and I said there wouldn't be any as far as I was concerned.

Sometime during my first week in Texas, Hardrock asked me to conduct a class on field stripping and maintenance of the .30-caliber machine gun, which I somehow accomplished to his satisfaction—though I am mechanically dysfunctional.

Ain't the Beer Cold!

On the way back to the barracks for lunch, Captain Green said, "Thompson, I don't know what trouble you've had but you don't have to worry about it here. Just fall in every morning for formation, then fall out and do whatever you want." So, I'd fall in, fall out, then head for the post exchange to occupy my time. Suddenly, Army duty was a snap.

I wasn't at Camp Howze very long when I had an opportunity to latch onto what may have been a permanent gravy train—if I had been swift enough to get aboard.

A Special Services captain, apparently aware of my civilian occupation, called me in and said, "We do a radio show here two days a week. Would you be interested in handling it?"

I explained to the captain I definitely would not be interested in doing any radio work for $78 a month (then my prevailing wage).

He smiled and replied, "Very well, Sergeant," and dismissed me.

About a week later, my orders were cut and I was soon on my way across the Atlantic Ocean on the *Queen Mary*, which had been converted from a stately oceanliner into a troop ship. All the way to Europe I was saying to myself, *"...not for 78 bucks a month."* Actually, I soon got a raise to $90 a month, but that was only because I was moving into a combat zone.

I guess the story shows that although the Good Lord gave me a reasonably good voice that has carried me all these years, he may have left me a little short when it came to brains.

I didn't spend too much time brooding over that dumb decision, however, because I did get to spend some time at home before shipping out (and, as you may later deduce, it was nine months later that Rose gave birth to our first child, Carol Lee—or, as we later called her, Sandy). In other words, the time at home was put to good use.

The *Queen Mary* undoubtedly had been a handsome ship in its prime, but it since had been stripped of its glitter and I didn't get to see much of it, anyway. I took an elevator directly to the promenade deck toward the bow, and was given a life preserver.

Just Call Me Sergeant

When I looked over the railing to see the guys still boarding, they looked pretty miniscule. I turned to another sergeant and said, "Instead of life preservers, maybe they should give us parachutes."

We left New York on January 8, 1945, and landed in Scotland some three and a half days later. We spent all our time aboard playing poker, drinking Cokes and eating Hershey bars, a familiar routine for Americans going to war. Looking back, it seems that we never even took time to sleep. I'm not able to win at solitaire, so you know how I did with competition.

We disembarked somewhere in Scotland and though it was January, I remember never being so impressed by the rich color of the grass along the Firth of Clyde (I don't think I was deceived by my color blindness).

We boarded a train and headed south with the shades drawn. We went through London to the English Channel, where we boarded an LST ship for a trip to the French port city of Le Havre.

We didn't exactly receive a heroes' welcome, or even a friendly greeting for being an ally. It seems the people of Le Havre had been warned by the Americans and British prior to D-Day (June 6, 1944) that they should evacuate the area before the German troops and ships in the harbor were bombed prior to the invasion. But the French failed to heed the warning and, as a result, suffered many casualties. So, when we disembarked, we were subjected to verbal abuse and even some rock and ice throwing.

My first stop on the continent was at a replacement depot (in GI language, a "repo-depot") in the Compiegne Forest. I listened very carefully as names were called, hoping to recognize one of the guys I met on the *Queen Mary*. Most of all, I was listening for my own name and assignment; neither of which was forthcoming.

Those who weren't called were loaded onto a "40 and 8" boxcar (so called because it had room for 40 servicemen and 8 horses). We traveled all night, standing up (with no horses), to a second repo-depot in Germany.

This time, I heard, "Thompson, sergeant, C.L., 30th Recon Troop." Mine was the only name called for that particular assignment and I started to think that when I turned down that captain's offer of a radio job in Texas, he decided to send me on some sort of suicide mission.

The name of my unit was something new to me, so I walked up to a sergeant and said, "Look, I'm not trying to be a wise guy, but exactly what is 'recon'?"

"See that guy over there?" he said, pointing to a nearby doorway. "He can tell you all you want to know."

I looked and could hardly believe my eyes. I later saw some dirty, tired looking people in combat, but this technical sergeant was as miserable looking as any I'd ever see. He would have been a perfect model for the GIs depicted by cartoonist Bill Mauldin in his popular wartime cartoon, "Willie and Joe."

The sergeant had been sent to pick me up, the lone member of the traveling party. He dumped out the contents of my duffel bag and, looking through his very small, coal-black eyes, said gruffly, "You ain't going to need none of that shit." He also threw away my gas mask, then got into the jeep and said, "Let's go."

As we drove along in the dark, artillery shells were exploding, the first shots I ever heard fired in anger, and every new sound terrified me.

We finally got to a town and he parked alongside what remained of a building. We went down to the cluttered cellar and there, lying on a pile of straw, was my new commander, Capt. James Humes of Richmond, who at that moment was reading a comic book. (Welcome to the war, rookie!)

I looked around the room and saw a rag-tag ensemble of human beings, whom I found out later had spent two days in combat capturing German pillboxes. They were more than a little tired...you might even say they were feeling a bit goofy.

This was my introduction to a combat area and the combat soldier. I learned later that this particular recon troop, along with other members of the 30th Division, had come ashore on the D-Day "Omaha Red" landing site.

They followed the 29th Division onto shore by four days, and the two divisions, along with 2nd Armored Division, for the most part spearheaded the drive through Northern Europe, through Dusseldorf and Cologne.

Captain Hume welcomed me to the 30th Recon Troop and said I'd be assigned to the "trains" (the name they used for head-quarters) a few days until I learned to operate all the radios and guns, and drive all the vehicles.

Newcomers also had to learn to distinguish the different voices, so they could identify them on the radio, but I don't recall ever operating a radio in code.

I spent weeks of training in code school, and was finally able to take 18 words a minute. But I never used a key once—it was all done by spoken word, most of which never came close to ac-cepted military procedure.

For example, if you were about to leave your position, it was usually, "Let's get the f___ out of here."

At this time, the Allies were still involved in the famed Battle of the Bulge, which was named for the sagging of the 80-mile battle front from Belgium through the Ardennes Forest when Hitler launched his last-ditch offensive.

I learned later that it was said to be the costliest battle in U.S. history, with 16,000 Americans killed and some 60,000 wounded. And, only at Bataan in the Philippines at the start of the war had more U.S. prisoners been surrendered.

The battle started on December 16, 1944, and it wasn't until January 31, 1945, that the Germans had been pushed back to where they had started the drive. The German losses of 100,000 killed or captured helped bring the war to a more rapid conclusion.

It was at the height of the Bulge, on December 22nd, when U.S. General Anthony McAuliffe answered a German com-mander's demand to surrender at Bastogne with the simple reply: "Nuts." Gen. George S. Patton's 3rd Army troops arrived in the area on December 26th after coming from the south, and the tide was soon turned.

The 30th Recon Troop had jeeps and vehicles called M8s, which were sort of light tanks with wheels and each carried a 37-milimeter cannon; on the ring mount was a 50-caliber machine gun which could cut through trees and was regarded as one of our better weapons in World War II. It spoke with authority, you might say.

When we were operating recon by fire, we'd pump off a few rounds from the machine gun, sending a message that we were in the area. We moved constantly, never staying in one place very long. The only time we stayed for a week or more was when the war ended and we were on occupation duty.

One day after a move, I decided to help Sgt. Buck Watson park some of the M8s. There was a lot of noise from artillery shells, but at this time there wasn't any in the immediate area.

We were backing the light tank between two houses (with no mirrors on the M8s, Watson was driving and I was waving directions) when I looked down the road 100 yards or more, and saw guys bailing out of trucks and running like crazy as the noise level increased. I asked what was going on and Watson said, "Just a little I.C."

I accepted that response and continued waving. Then I said, "What's I.C.?"

"Incoming," was his matter-of-fact response, and we again resumed parking the M8.

But I was still puzzled and said, "Incoming what?"

"Artillery, you stupid baldheaded S.O.B."

This time, Watson pierced my mental fog and he had to park that sucker himself after I took off for the cellar. That was my first experience of being close to combat and I don't imagine I reacted any differently than any other rookie.

I was with the third platoon of the 30th Recon, commanded by Lt. Chet Prentiss, who didn't fit the perceived notion of a combat officer. He was a graduate of the University of Pennsylvania's Wharton School of Business with a very slight build (5-10, 140 pounds), a pale complexion, blue eyes, and curly black hair—something like a Little Lord Fauntleroy. But he was a decent man and a top officer who had one habit we all appreciated.

Whenever we posted a roadblock at an intersection or particular point on the map, we'd spread six jeeps and three M8s over the designated area. This was usually done under the cover of darkness.

Everytime we launched such an operation, Prentiss and his jeep driver, Cpl. Marshall Reddig, would venture out about a mile in front of us. If the enemy was out there, Prentiss and Reddig would attract some fire and we'd have to change our plans.

I remember that we were leaving our prescribed area only once, when Prentiss and Reddig encountered a German Tiger tank as they inched along with their jeep in "creeper gear."

We were told later that Reddig had made a left turn and was going up a slight grade, when Prentiss saw the tank. The Germans, in turn, had either heard or seen our guys and prepared to fire. But their old tank didn't have an automatic turret, so they had to crank the 88-milimeter cannon into place.

It seemed to be a good time to depart and Prentiss jumped just as Reddig hit the accelerator and made a sharp right-handed turn. The lieutenant landed in the back, head down, with one leg sticking up, and that's how they came speeding back to our outpost. It looked like something we'd later see on the hit TV show, "M*A*S*H."

Reddig, who was a bit raucous like the late Baltimore legend Charlie Eckman, was nicknamed, "Whisperer."

After enjoying that bit of slap-stick humor, it was the consensus of opinion that we'd better move back a little, and we did.

In a history of the (Old Hickory) 30th Division, published after the war, it was explained that the normal mission of the recon troop was to maintain contact and security between scattered elements of the 30th and an adjacent division, as well as maintaining roadblocks.

Although almost as strong as a rifle company, the recon troop rarely was used as infantry because of the specialized abilities of its members and because so many were tied down to vehicles and radios.

After successfully crossing the Ruhr River, we continued on to the Rhine. One day along the banks of the Rhine, Sgt. Buck Watson and I were repairing some wire when an artillery shell burst above us. When that happens, shrapnel scatters at maybe a 45-degree angle while there is nothing but concussion felt directly under the burst.

That's what Buck and I felt. I was thrown into a ditch and Buck was rolled over. Fortunately, we weren't anywhere near the jeep, which took the greater part of the explosion and was ripped to shreds.

After assuring one another that we were OK, we looked down the road to see an ambulance on the way. The guys at platoon headquarters had witnessed the explosion and had dispatched a meatwagon to pick up what they figured were our remains. Our ears were ringing and bleeding a little; otherwise we were fine.

On another occasion, I was coming back to the house we lived in when I was pinned down against a big stone wall in the barnyard area. A shell hit nearby in a cobblestone street, caromed into a field, and never exploded. I got up, ran across the street, and dove into the cellar. If the shell had exploded, who knows what would have happened.

In retrospect, those two incidents convinced me that fate was doing more than merely deciding my career in broadcasting. It also was making certain I would be able to resume that career at the end of the war.

Toward the end of the war, we were in a German farmhouse overnight. Surrounding the house was a wall about 10 to 12 feet tall, with two wooden gates in front. All our vehicles were in this area, not outside in the street.

All the guys in the platoon were tired so "Squeaky" Gaddis, who came from headquarters with our mail, volunteered to stand guard while we slept. Lieutenant Prentiss accepted the offer and told Gaddis to stand in the turret of the M8 and if he heard anything he couldn't identify, just awaken us.

It was getting near daylight when Gaddis heard some strange noises on the cobblestone street. He knew we were in the house, so it couldn't be anyone out there who would be friendly. Taking no chances, "Squeaky" pulled the pin on a grenade and tossed the explosive into the street.

Just Call Me Sergeant

That got us up in a hurry. Thinking we were in combat, we grabbed our weapons and rushed from the house. No one wanted to stick his head over the wall to check and because it was still dark, we couldn't see anything from the attic window.

We still had about an hour to go before daylight so all we could do was to listen. If there were any Germans out there, let them open the gate; we weren't going to make the first move. We were under our vehicles, in case grenades were thrown. We listened so hard, our ears hurt.

Finally, with the first light of dawn we took a look...and saw a cow in the middle of the street that "Squeaky" had killed. We were not very popular after slaying the lone milk supply of the townspeople, but we left the area shortly thereafter, realizing that in a hour we had gone from sheer terror to some of the best laughter the recon troop had had for a long time. Somebody designed a homemade medal and presented it to our hero, "Squeaky" Gaddis.

As we neared the Rhine, we realized something unusual was taking place with the 30th Division, which was located about as far north as any American troops had gone, right next to the British.

On the banks of the Rhine we noticed that no one below the rank of full colonel, even from our headquarters, was allowed to come into our area. When food was brought from the "trains," we had to go back to a given spot for the marmight cans (sort of oversized thermos containers) used to keep the food warm. After we ate, the cans were returned the same way.

We didn't wear any 30th Division patches on our uniforms and any identification marks on our vehicles were either covered with mud or in some way rendered illegible so that German observation posts on the other side of the Rhine wouldn't know the 30th Division was in the area.

The Germans were well aware of the 29th and 30th's role in the drive across Europe, so if they spotted either unit in the area, they'd figure that's where the crossing of the Rhine could be expected.

Later, when I was part of an advance detachment of the 30th Division going back to the States aboard the S.S. *Sea Robin* and ticketed for duty in the Pacific against the Japanese, a Lieutenant Tomlinson told me *the rest of the story.*

Tomlinson said, and it was later confirmed in the published 30th Division records, that in addition to obliterating 30th Division markings in our area, a false front actually was established elsewhere to mislead the Germans into thinking that was where the 30th was located.

With the Germans looking for an attack opposite the false front, the casualties were extremely low when we made the crossing in our area.

I got to know Tomlinson as a Special Services officer. Often, when we were resting, he'd bring us candy and soap, and mail on occasion. While we were on the banks of the Rhine, he followed the 30th Division signs, even though he felt he wasn't going in the right direction. He finally reached a sign for the 30th Recon, approached a sergeant he didn't recognize and asked to see Captain Hume.

Tomlinson was directed to a house, where the officer behind a desk said he was Captain Hume.

"You're not the Captain Hume I know," Tomlinson said.

"Sit down, Lieutenant, and we'll talk a little bit," the officer responded, and then explained the elaborate deception.

While along the Rhine, Americans occupied a castle owned by an exporter of wines and after blowing down the door to the wine cellar, we carried away cases of the bubbly on our M8s and jeeps.

About that time, the guys in our unit started to feel sorry for themselves for not getting any leave time in Paris. I was a Johnny-come-lately, but some of those who had been around a long time said, "Let's go to Paris."

We started out but one guy in the unit who didn't drink, a minister's son, reminded Lieutenant Prentiss that this would be desertion in the face of the enemy. Prentiss agreed, so we returned to our old positions.

Then we were really P.O.'d because apparently no one missed us or knew we were gone. There was so much traffic backed up, waiting to cross the Rhine, we probably could have made Paris if we hadn't chickened out.

After the crossing, the war was just about over...and it did end as we reached the Elbe River at Magdeburg. Then the only mission remaining for a recon troop was a contact mission to join up with the Russians advancing from the other direction.

Knowing the war was over, this was the kind of assignment that was not meant for volunteers. Who knows, people in the area might still be jittery and some gunfire might be exchanged because of a misunderstanding. As it turned out, we didn't have to run the contact mission; that job fell to another recon unit.

According to the post-war records, the 30th Recon Troop took 3,504 prisoners in Europe, and I was involved in the capture of just one of those. Well, it wasn't really much of a capture...he just swam up to us on the river bank and capitulated.

The 19 of us in the platoon were spread out over a two-mile front. Under normal combat conditions, that would have been a nervous situation. We all knew that the war was over, but we still had to maintain a sense of military readiness.

I was sitting out one night with Cpl. "Gibby" Gibbons, and it was pretty cold even though it was spring. Gibby heard something, so we stopped talking and listened.

Son-of-a-gun, if a German soldier didn't come out of the water, rattling and shaking from the cold water and turning a bit blue. No problem; he had achieved his personal objective by contacting a couple of Americans, not Russians.

Gibby told Lieutenant Prentiss, who said take the prisoner back to headquarters. Gibby put the guy in the back of the jeep, without a blanket, and drove him back. Chalk up another prisoner for the 30th Recon!

So, we were on the banks of Elbe River when the VE Day (victory in Europe) celebration was in full swing in Paris. I was told it was *one of the wildest and glorious celebrations of victory in the history of victories.*

Among those taking part was one of the best football and baseball announcers I've ever heard, the very likeable guy from

Ain't the Beer Cold!

Tennessee, the late Lindsey Nelson, who later became my friend and preceded me into the Broadcasters' Wing at the Baseball Hall of Fame in Cooperstown.

He and the Pulitzer Prize-winning war correspondent, Ernie Pyle, were standing in front of a hotel when the celebration started. Champagne and cognac were flowing, while the GIs were partying with innumerable citizens, mostly women. Music was playing and they danced, paraded and jumped up and down on the hoods of vehicles, grabbing and hugging one another.

In the midst of the jubilation, I was told, Ernie turned to Lindsey and said something that has stuck with me all these years: "Linds, any man out there who sleeps by himself tonight is an exhibitionist."

Never have I forgotten those words of Ernie Pyle, who later lost his life in the war in the Pacific. I never knew the man, but I'm glad I got to know him indirectly through Lindsey.

After hostilities ceased, units that had fought in the north were moved to the south for occupation duties, and those who advanced through the south were moved to the north. The switches were made to head off possible retaliation by Germans who may have harbored bitter feelings about units they had encountered.

As a result, the 30th Division was sent south and I found myself in the Hartz Mountains near the Czechoslovakian border, an absolutely gorgeous site for occupation duty.

There was one disturbing thing...quite a few German soldiers who were still armed refused to surrender to the Russians, and wanted to surrender to the Americans or British.

In the mountains around Falkenstein we had to ride perimeter patrols. It was pretty quiet usually, but the patrols were still necessary in case some Germans did not want to surrender.

I was back in Le Havre, on the first leg of my trip back to the States, when the French celebrated Bastille Day on July 14th, their independence day. It was quite an experience hearing thousands of Frenchmen sing an emotional rendition of their national anthem, "The Marseillaise."

We departed Le Havre on July 20th aboard the S.S. *Sea*

Just Call Me Sergeant

Robin, a welded-hull Liberty ship, and arrived back in the good ole U.S.A. on July 28th. I was in the advance detachment of the 30th Division which was sent to Fort Jackson near Columbia, South Carolina. While there, waiting for eventual assignment to the Pacific for the war against Japan, I worked part-time at WIS Radio in the evenings. I replaced a lieutenant who was going back to work at WCAU in Philadelphia after his discharge. I'd do my regular Army duties during the day, then head to the station after retreat. After doing a newscast at 6 o'clock, I'd play records and give station breaks up until the 11 P.M. newscast. I'd be sure to mention on the air the names of some of the Fort Jackson officers like wishing them a happy birthday.

I was home on furlough when the first atom bomb was dropped on Hiroshima on August 6, 1945 (and Harry Truman went to the top of the list of my favorite presidents), and a few days later we celebrated VJ Day, the end of World War II. Like any other town in the United States or all over the free world, Reading had a wild and wonderful celebration. Rose and I went downtown to join in.

What comes around, goes around...and I found myself back at Indiantown Gap to be honorably discharged. Believe it or not, as I viewed others in the happy group, the only guy I recognized was Kenny Sensenig. I hadn't seen him since we both were inducted one year, eight months, and 29 days earlier.

I was credited with six months and 21 days of foreign duty and was discharged with a service medal which included three bronze stars for the Rhineland, Ardennes, and Central Europe campaigns.

My family was going to pick me up in town because the base would have been too congested with so many relatives on hand to greet the soon-to-be civilians. So I took a bus downtown and went into a soda fountain across the street to await my ride.

I carried an envelope with my discharge papers and was wearing my "ruptured duck" pin which signified my discharge. As I sat at the counter, the waitress asked what I wanted and I replied, "a cherry Coke."

Ain't the Beer Cold!

I was sipping away when she walked from behind the counter, put a nickel in the juke box (yes, it was only a nickel in those days), and said she was playing the song for me. I had gone through combat service unscathed and was back to take my place in the field of commercial radio again. The recording couldn't have been more appropo as Frank Sinatra sang:

"I've got the world on a string, sitting on a rainbow, got the string around my finger..."

Chapter 7

My Debut in the Major Leagues

Nobody is ever happy about going to war. But since we were involved in one, I was proud to have been able to serve my country in its hour of stress.

In peacetime, we probably don't think too much about service to our country and we complain bitterly about a million and one things that seem to be wrong with our way of life. But still, with all of its faults, the U.S.A. is still the greatest nation in the world.

But enough post-war reflection; it was time to return to broadcasting. Not only did I get my job back at WIBG in Philadelphia, I also was given a substantial raise to a salary of more than $50 a week that represented a noteworthy milestone in my career. And that didn't include our many perks.

One of the most enjoyable fringe benefits was being able to watch the women office workers walking down Walnut Street at the end of a day's work on their way to catch the subway at Broad Street.

Someone wrote that between four and five o'clock on any weekday afternoon more beautiful women passed that location than on any other block in the world. As a willing witness, I hereby testify to the truth of that statement.

Many of our employees who didn't have work to do, or at

least were not on the air at the time, would come downstairs about 4:15, lean up against the wall of the WIBG building, and just watch the impromptu parade. It was a sight to behold, and the repetition never became boring.

But the WIBG gang was not alone in this *pulsating perusal of pulchritude*. A lot of other guys came out of other offices at that hour and the drugstore across the street used to empty every day at about 4:15 for the same reason.

But the most beautiful vision of all was the boss' daughter, Grace, who visited the station about once a week or so (John B. Kelly was there only once or twice a week, himself) and walked up the stairs to Dad's office. Before ascending the last flight, she had to walk past the studio.

I worked out an early warning system with our telephone operator, who would call me in the studio to warn that *Grace was on her way*. The alert gave me time to make certain the record would last long enough so I could get into position to watch Grace ascend the stairs, walk down the hall, and up the next flight. Grace always waved as she went past and her radiant smile was an added bonus. Talk about perks!

I never managed to see her leave, probably because I wasn't tipped in advance about her departure. In fact, as far as I knew she may have taken the elevator down. But I'll never forget that entrance.

A contrasting but spectacular exit on those same stairs, was also memorable for a different reason.

Announcer Paul Collins was a small, good-looking guy with a great head of hair that he spent a lot of time combing. He also had a great sense of humor, a trait that I severely tested one night with a devious practical joke.

Paul ended his shift every night at 8:30. When he finished, he had to sprint from the station, down Walnut Street to Broad and across to Penn Station to catch the last train to his home in the suburbs.

On this particular night, I decided to set a booby trap with the folding chairs which were often used for audiences in the studio where the dance band performed. I carried as many chairs as I could down the stairs to the first landing and piled them about three feet deep at that point and about half that high on the stairs leading to the next level below. A lot of trips were required.

As usual Paul signed off, didn't say a word to anyone, and made his nightly Dagwood Bumstead dash for the door. It was clear sailing for the first flight but when he turned left at the landing, I can tell you there were chairs rattling for a long time.

Needless to say, Paul missed his train that night after crashing into my barrier and for a day or two, I was hailed as King of the Hill (or, you might say, King of the Steps).

But Paul wasn't always on the butt end of the jokes. He was the resident genius behind a form of distraction that equaled those flaming waste cans that were eased into place behind on-air announcers. He would inflate one of those long, narrow balloons, write a message on a piece of paper, tape it to the balloon, and float it past the window where the announcer was performing. The message might include the announcer's name and some terrible things about his ancestry, his family, or friends.

You even had to be alert when simply walking through a doorway. You just didn't barge on through; you had to be careful to open the door just a crack to make certain no paper cups of water had been taped on the door jam, awaiting a sudden movement that would send them crashing down on your head.

With all the hijinks, we had a great staff of broadcasters with diverse personalities, including Collins, Tommy Moore, Ray Walton, Bob Knox, Fred Whiting, Roy Hinkle (or Roy Neal), who later covered NASA space shots for NBC. All were under the direction of program director Doug Arthur.

We had certain rules we had to follow, including a ban on cussing. If someone couldn't resist and let go an expletive, he had to donate a quarter to the "Cuss Pot." I think we used the proceeds at the end of the year to buy a round of drinks.

Our station was in the midst of "Radio Row" on Walnut Street, along with competitors WCAU and KYW. All the stations used to play jokes on one another and I used to go to WCAU frequently in the afternoons to listen to Jan Savitt's house band in rehearsal.

Stan Lee Broza, who used to host the "Horn and Hardart Kiddie Hour" and was the program director for WCAU, was frequently at odds with Paul Douglas, their free-spirited sports guy.

Every night when WCAU went off the air, they broadcast a missing person's report. One night, Paul listed Stan as a missing person and described him perfectly by age, height, and weight, and said he was last seen on Walnut Street.

Somebody in the business heard the report and the news spread like wildfire among the radio stations. Obviously, Stan and the other WCAU people didn't hear it, mainly because there aren't many executives who stay up until 1:30 or 1:45 A.M. to hear the station sign off.

So, the missing person report was repeated the following night and all the radio guys in town were tuned in. But when it was broadcast a third time, Paul was caught...and fired.

That didn't faze the local hero, who eventually wound up in Hollywood. There he co-starred with Judy Holliday when she won an Academy Award for her role in *Born Yesterday* and played a catcher in *It Happens Every Spring*, the baseball spoof about a college professor (Ray Milland) and the wood-repellant substance which made his pitches unhittable.

Part of the fun in working at WIBG was going to dinner with three or four of the broadcasters while Doug Arthur conducted his "Danceland" show between 6 and 7:30 P.M.

Most of the time we went to Horn and Hardart, particularly when the automat came along. I guess we were fascinated by placing coins into the wall slots which opened the window locks and allowed us to reach the food. It was a new experience, and the prices were right.

About once a week, probably on pay day, we would have a cocktail before dinner. Then we would go to Duffy's Tavern, where a former major on the staff of SHAEF (Supreme Headquarters Allied Expeditionary Forces) in Europe worked as the bartender and was also part-owner.

My Debut in the Major Leagues

We had a running bet with the bartender. He said no matter how many drinks we ordered (in those days, Manhattans were pretty popular), he would pour from the cocktail shaker and fill all our glasses right to the brim. If not, the drinks were on the house.

Of all our trips to Duffy's, I think we had just one round of free drinks before realizing that we had virtually no chance. We even checked for any sign of trickery but it was uncanny the way he could mix just enough liquid and ice to bring it out dead even.

For me, another plus for working in Philadelphia was being able to listen to some great music at Willie Krechmer's bar, not far from the station. On Monday nights, some of the greatest names in modern music would appear for a jam session—such artists as Harry James, Benny Goodman, Louie Armstrong, and Gene Krupa.

My roots in jazz and big band music ran deep, back to the nights I worked on a milk truck in Palmer, Massachusetts, as a teenager. When we drove up to the dairy to load the truck, a radio station in Hartford would always play Ella Fitzgerald's "A-Tisket, A-Tasket" record somewhere between 1:00 and 1:30 and I'd make my cousin wait until the record was finished before we went to work.

Despite all the diversions, there was plenty to keep me busy on the job. I recently found an article that had been torn out of a magazine called the *Radio Mirror* and saved by my father. After Dad died, I inherited a lot of his papers. The story tells about me doing two daily sports shows, plus college football, Warriors pro basketball, and Flyers hockey, baseball during the summer with Byrum Saam, and a couple of boxing matches.

I even had my first experience with NFL football and it made a lasting impression on me. Greasy Neale, coach of the Philadelphia Eagles at the time, asked if I wanted to visit the sidelines during an exhibition game. It was OK with me and I got final permission from Saam, who was doing the play-by-play.

But after 10 minutes or so, in the days before face masks, I had heard enough screaming, grunting, and assorted horrible noises to last a lifetime. I tapped Greasy on the arm and said, "Thanks a lot."

Ain't the Beer Cold!

"Giving up, kid?" he asked.

"Yeh," I responded and left before he had a chance to shame me out of my decision.

The magazine article included a photo taken outside of WIBG's picture window, with a crowd standing on the sidewalk watching the sports show in progress. It was from that show window studio that I once interviewed actor Edward Everett Horton, who frequently played light comedy roles, sometimes as a butler or the best friend of the male lead.

Under the format of the show, people who were appearing in Philadelphia stage shows would drop in to do an interview and, of course, plug the play.

Horton was fantastic, just incredible. With his quick wit and storytelling ability, he was a great interview and the repartee drew a crowd that steadily grew in size. Traffic came to a standstill, with trolley cars clang-clang-clanging to get through. Finally, mounted police had to be called to disperse the assemblage on Walnut Street.

After he returned to Hollywood, Horton sent me a gift of a necktie and matching handkerchief. That interview was clearly the highlight of my career as a studio announcer.

I also conducted a memorable interview with film actress Sylvia Sydney that was at first interrupted by nasty comments made by her husband. We finally solved that problem by moving the husband to another room, away from the microphone.

But it was sports that proved to be my niche. Les Quailey got me into football very quickly that first year back from the service. I did Temple football play-by-play on Friday or Saturday night, and loved every minute of it.

On occasion, I went to Franklin Field to do color on a Penn game with Saam doing play-by-play. At a Penn-Cornell game around Thanksgiving, I asked Saam what we could do for half-time. He said, "Why not go downstairs and get Granny?"

"Granny?"

"Yeh, Grantland Rice."

To me, that was like saying, "Go talk to Babe Ruth," and my timidity apparently showed.

My Debut in the Major Leagues

"He's a good guy," Saam said. "He won't bite your head off."

So I went down to the press box, recognized Rice, told him I was working with Saam and invited him to be a halftime guest. He accepted and proved to be just as fluid with the spoken word as he was in print. I could ask him anything about the game and he'd just pick up the ball and roll right along.

I was in his company once or twice after that, but my best memory of Rice has been recalling his book, *The Tumult and the Shouting*, clearly my all-time favorite sports volume.

I still go back to that book every now and then for my reading pleasure or to use what Granny wrote about the death of Ring Lardner when I'm preparing a eulogy for one of my friends.

Writers in those days used to write poetry and Granny was one of the best. He covered just about every sports event and was one of the most respected and beloved newspaper columnists of all time. It was a thrill to first encounter a living legend in such an off-beat manner and, let me tell you, he carried me during that halftime show.

I didn't just seek out celebrities, however. I also took advantage of average, everyday fans in the stands when they could offer some help to a struggling announcer.

My first attempt at doing play-by-play in hockey was in the second game I ever saw in that sport. Our broadcast booth at the arena was over one of the entrances, surrounded by spectators.

I've always operated on the theory that if I don't know something, then for goodness' sake, ask questions...just don't try to fool the listeners.

So when the hockey game got underway there was a whistle on the ice and I wasn't too sure what it was for. I turned around, microphone in hand, and asked the guy behind me the reason for the whistle, and he told me the infraction was "icing." I thanked him, then asked his name and where he lived.

Another whistle and this time I asked a guy sitting beside me and went through the same routine. After a few games, the first tickets sold were those around my booth and the fans gave me some valuable on-the-job training.

Ain't the Beer Cold!

It was a unique experience, to say the least. The fans could have torn me to ribbons, assuming that the guy behind the mike should know what he's doing. But rather than ridicule me or try to confuse, they somehow felt this was special...plus they were getting their names on the air.

The memory of how helpful people can be will stay with me forever. I've found that throughout my career more people have tried to help rather than hurt me, wherever I've gone. That's why I feel that people, particularly those in Baltimore, helped carry me into the Baseball Hall of Fame and I guess it all started with those hockey fans in Philadelphia.

I certainly was more familiar with baseball than the game of hockey. But I didn't anticipate my sudden introduction to play-by-play on the final day of the 1946 season when broadcasters Byrum Saam and Claude Haring missed the Shibe Park elevator back to the press level after being honored on the field between games of a doubleheader.

I somehow passed that instant audition and when the basketball season began, I started covering high school games when station owner John B. Kelly landed a contract with Coca-Cola.

Kelly figured if I could keep up with the fast pace of basketball, I could do horse racing. He wanted me to go to Florida and learn the ropes by sitting with race callers all the way up the Eastern Seaboard.

With that training, he thought I could do the race of the day on WCAU, Monday through Friday, from the track at Atlantic City, where he was chairman of the board. On Saturday, I'd do the feature race on the CBS Radio Network.

That was the boss' wish for me in 1947 and the idea had me more excited than when I got the call that got me out of Youngstown. I couldn't wait to tell Doug Arthur.

But Doug, who met with me at the end of each year to review my career moves, quieted me down and explained patiently that the N.W. Ayer Agency was thinking about using me on baseball in 1947.

It didn't take me very long to figure out that a baseball season

My Debut in the Major Leagues

lasted a lot longer than a race meeting, not to mention I knew something about the game. So I opted for baseball.

In addition, I didn't realize it at the time but race callers must rely on saddle silks to identify the horses and I would have been a colossal flop because of my green-gray color deficiency.

While I felt flattered that my boss was impressed enough to offer me a special job, I was elated that Les Quailey and the N.W. Ayer Agency were convinced that I deserved a shot with baseball.

The long, winding road to Cooperstown began in earnest with the 1947 season and we had the best job in baseball. We covered all the Athletics and Phillies home games at Shibe Park and never had to go on the road.

Saam was a great guy to work with, and he was a noted softball pitcher around Philadelphia. He had been a football quarterback at Texas Christian, but he didn't get to play much. He had a guy ahead of him by the name of Sammy Baugh.

Haring, my other partner in the booth, always called me "Moose," because of my ample nose, and for some reason I don't remember, I called him "Yonko."

I bought my first automobile in 1947, a two-door green sedan, and after a series of weird events I was convinced that green was my unlucky color (remember my colorblindness).

In those days, there was no secure parking lot for the media at Shibe Park, so I parked on the street. Before the baseball season was half over, someone driving up Lehigh Street ripped the left rear fender off my car.

I took the car back to the dealer and the repairs were handled by the insurance company. The following winter I was driving from Philadelphia to Reading when someone who had borrowed a car without the owner's permission ran a stop sign and hit my refurbished vehicle broadside, knocked me across three lanes of the road and onto a railing. Back for more insurance-paid repairs.

The crowning blow to my Green Hex came after a Phillies' home game was rained out and we were on our way back to the studio to do a telegraphic reconstruction of an Athletics' road game.

Ain't the Beer Cold!

It was raining as we headed southbound on 15th Street, and about a block and a half ahead I could see a horse-drawn cart standing idle at a side street. Just as we passed that intersection, something startled the horse. It raced out and leaped into the right side of the car, hitting the metal stanchion that separated the front and rear windows.

If the car had been traveling a little faster or slower, the horse's hoof would have gone through one of the windows. But Saam, who was seated in front, and telegrapher Harry Simon, on the right side in the back seat, both escaped injury.

The horse also survived, but this third incident convinced me it was time for a change and it wasn't long before I traded in my Mean Green Machine.

I've retained the memory of those episodes, however, and most of my friends have heard them. I usually brought them up when it was time to rent a car during spring training.

Year after year, traveling secretary Phil Itzoe of the Orioles would ask me what kind of car I wanted and my answer would always be the same: "I don't much care, as long as it has room in the trunk for two sets of golf clubs...and it isn't green."

One time, however, there was a green car awaiting me in Fort Lauderdale. But Itzoe was so accommodating and had gone to so much trouble, I decided to keep it.

As I checked the car's equipment before leaving the darkened airport, I reached under the dashboard and pulled on what I thought was the brake release...and the hood flew open. Phil and my wife Rose, who had been exchanging knowing glances about the color of the car, burst into laughter and I joined in after realizing it was my mistake and had nothing to do with the hex. But enough of colors and cars, let's get back to baseball.

I've been in the broadcast booth for several no-hitters during my career, but my first one left me literally gasping for breath.

It was thrown in 1947 by Bill McCahan of the Athletics against the Washington Senators. The only batter to reach base was Stan Spence, who was safe at first after first baseman Ferris Fain fielded his grounder and threw wildly to McCahan covering the bag. Elmer Valo made a great catch in the outfield to preserve the no-no.

My Debut in the Major Leagues

I had to read commercials between innings and as the tension of the no-hitter mounted, I found it difficult to control myself and to breathe normally.

By the bottom of the eighth inning, I was hanging onto the railing in front of the booth, just hypnotized and totally unable to do my job as a professional broadcaster. I was so engrossed, I couldn't comprehend what was happening. So Saam, in addition to doing the play-by-play with Haring, took over my job, too.

I had much better control in later years when I covered no-hitters by Hoyt Wilhelm (working with Bill Veeck on a regional NBC-TV game), Tom Phoebus and Jim Palmer of the Orioles, and another against the O's by Nolan Ryan of the California Angels.

The no-hitter by Ryan was one of seven in his long and distinguished career. The last batter of the game was Bobby Grich, who fouled off three or four fastballs with a 3-2 count before fanning at a slider down and away. Grich was furious after the game, wondering how Ryan could throw a slider in that situation.

Ryan's post-game ovation was thunderous. Right in the middle of it, Nolan left the field, went into the boxseats, kissed his wife, and led her onto the field to share in the moment. I thought that was a class touch.

Now, back to Philadelphia. As far as I recall now, the three of us split the play-by-play most of the time, with Saam doing five innings, and Haring and I two apiece.

Sometime during my two years of broadcasting major league games in Philadelphia, I became aware of Pete Adellis, a guy whom you might call a professional rooter.

He never used any abusive or foul language, but he had rooting down to a science and had the kind of voice you could hear all over the ballpark.

Adellis, who later went to work in the Phillies' ticket office, I think, did his best heckling from the photographers' overhang on the mezzanine level at Shibe Park. He would sit there and bellow the same phrase over and over in his piercing voice.

"Walk him Walter...walk him Walter," he would yell to Washington pitcher Walter Masterson. He'd go on for innings until

Ain't the Beer Cold!

Masterson would begin to look up and vent his anger by gestering and hollering on his own. Upsetting the pitcher was Adellis' aim and when he had accomplished his mission, he left, feeling very satisfied with himself.

Once, when the A's were playing in Cleveland, Indians outfielder Larry Doby misplayed a flyball or lost it in the sun and the ball hit Doby on his head or shoulder. Just like that, the heckler had a new target.

Adellis read about Doby's mishap in the paper and the next time the Indians came into Shibe, Adellis was ready. From the overhang just below the radio booth, he started: "Hey, Dopey...hey, Dopey," and to emphasize the point he was wearing a World War I German helmet with "Dopey" lettered across the front.

The needling continued and Doby, a left-handed batter, finally asked for time and looked up to the third-base overhang. The moment he looked, Adellis grabbed a hammer and clanged the helmet several times. Everyone laughed, including Doby.

I can still recall the A's starting lineup in those days: Ferris Fain at first, Pete Suder at second, Eddie Joost at shortstop, Hank Majeski at third, with Elmer Valo, Sam Chapman, and Barney McCosky in the outfield from right to left, with Buddy Rosar the catcher.

One of the pitchers that first year was Joe Coleman, who later pitched for the Orioles in 1954-55, and Billy Hitchcock, who played a lot of second base in 1948, later was to manage the Orioles in 1962-63.

McCosky was a heck of a good average hitter (.328 in 1947 and .326 in 1948), but he didn't drive in many runs (52 and 46 in the two years I covered the A's).

I was told a story (I don't know if it was true) that when McCosky went to bat with a man in scoring position, manager Connie Mack would take a $50 bill out of his pocket and wave it while looking toward the plate. He seldom had to turn over one of the bills to McCosky.

Chapman, a good fielder and hitter who lost almost four years

My Debut in the Major Leagues

because of service in World War II, for some reason took me under his wing. He would sit next to me in the dugout during batting practice, telling me about the batters' tendencies in the box and how they were pitched to.

He'd do that once or twice a week. For someone just beginning, having a major league player talk to me as though I were another player, was really something special and an experience I'll take with me forever.

Lou Brissie, also a war veteran, had a metal plate in one of his legs but that didn't stop the big left-handed pitcher from competing, and competing well. He compiled a 14-10 record in 1948 and was 16-11 the next season after I had gone to Baltimore.

Brissie, pitching the first game of a Patriots' Day doubleheader in Boston, was hit on his "bad" leg by a line drive off the bat of Ted Williams and was knocked down.

Teddy Ballgame almost didn't run to first base and once he got there, he turned and made a beeline to the mound because he was so concerned, as was everyone else. I wasn't there to see it, but Ted's genuine concern for a fellow player made an impression on me.

Ferris Fain was a pretty good hitter, twice winning the American League batting championship at .344 in 1951 and .327 the next year. But he was not as efficient as a fielder, making anywhere from 13 to 22 errors a year at first base. Sometimes, when he fielded a grounder and prepared to throw for a play at the plate, Mack would yell, "Look out, he's got it again."

Who could get angry with Connie Mack, the kindly gentleman who managed the A's for *50 years* while wearing a business suit and tie in the dugout?

Byrum Saam first introduced me to Mack in the clubhouse. The venerable skipper didn't like to go out and make speeches, but if you got to him when the players were on the field working out, he was very affable and outgoing.

But he also had a temper. One day, in a game against the St. Louis Browns, Mack was upset over a decision. He called time and waved for umpire Art Pasarella to come over to the dugout.

Ain't the Beer Cold!

When Pasarella arrived and leaned in the dugout, Mack grabbed him by the neck and shook vigorously.

Pasarella never flinched, remained calm with a sense of dignity and didn't say a word. I thought he must be a pretty good umpire to understand the frustration of this elderly citizen and was big enough to let him vent that frustration which had no bearing on the ballgame. It was just a professional performance.

Mack also fired Nelson Potter in 1948, the year he pitched for three teams. Standing on the dugout steps, Mack said: "Take off your uniform...you're through."

Excuse me for digressing about Mack; I still had another story about Ferris Fain, one that he told on himself about going out on the town while the A's were playing in Washington.

Ferris was dancing with a young lady when another guy wanted to cut in. "Burrhead" Fain objected. One word led to another and as Ferris recalled, "I hit this kid with the best punch I'd ever thrown.

"When the kid got off the floor and started back at me, I knew I was going to get the worst beating I'd ever gotten in my life."

Fain's adversary happened to be engaged to the woman he was with on the dance floor, and Ferris wound up in the hospital with a displaced shoulder.

Over in the National League, the "Whiz Kids" were beginning to take shape for the Phillies, leading to a championship in 1950.

My favorite player was Andy Seminick, a rugged physical specimen behind the plate who was involved in the shortest fight I ever saw in baseball. It happened after Gene Hermanski of the Dodgers was blocked at the plate and tagged out by Seminick.

Hermanski came up swinging...and it was short and sweet. Seminick took one step back, shredded his mitt as if he were taking mud off his left hand, threw one punch and Hermanski went face down on the plate. Never saw one equal to that in all my days of covering games.

Robin Roberts was a rookie for the Phils in my last year at Philadelphia, on his way to 286 wins and a place in the Hall of

My Debut in the Major Leagues

Fame. He earned 42 of those victories with the Orioles from 1962 to 1965.

Robin provided me with two memorable anecdotes, one an off-the-field yarn involving yours-truly and the other about the fiery Hall-of-Famer, Jackie Robinson.

When the Orioles went on the road to play a game in Kansas City, the traveling party stayed at a hotel just across the Missouri River, on the Kansas side. When we went to the ballpark, we had to cross the river, where the stench from the nearby stockyards would make you want to hold your breath all the way across the bridge.

All the noise and chatter on the bus would stop when you got the first whiff of the stockyards. One time, we were in the middle of the bridge, hoping to cross as quickly as possible, when Robin pierced the silence:

"It's times like this that I feel sorry for that poor S.O.B. Thompson (referring to the amount of air that I could inhale through my ample honker)."

Robin also tells a story about Robinson, who integrated the major leagues in my rookie 1947 season and was just unbelieveable. He seemed to explode when he started to run, and didn't need many steps to reach full speed.

If he were picked off, it seemed he just wanted to be caught in a rundown because about the only way to tag him was to first make a flying tackle.

Anyway, Robin said he once hit the stretch position, with his hands at his belt, and looked toward second to see Jackie already down around the shortstop position. After they stared at one another, Robin straddled the rubber and Jackie never moved.

Robin walked off the mound toward Jackie, who remained motionless while waiting for the pitcher to commit himself with a throw and start a rundown. But Robin continued walking, ignoring Jackie as he faked one way, then the other, until he merely reached out and made the tag. He swears it's a true story!

After the 1948 baseball season, I had my surprise on-air audition at the Navy-Missouri football game in Baltimore. Then Doug

Ain't the Beer Cold!

Arthur gave me my annual assessment and it was his feeling that I wasn't going to make much advancement in Philadelphia as long as Saam was active.

While I was deciding what to do, my other old mentor, Les Quailey, came to my rescue. He tipped me that the N.W. Ayer Agency, which had the rights to both International League baseball and Navy football, was looking for someone for both jobs, replacing Bill Dyer on the Orioles' broadcasts.

As an aside, I feel obliged to mention that the Phils and A's eventually did have separate broadcasting crews. The agency wanted Saam to stay with the A's, apparently out of deference to Connie Mack, the team's aging manager, so Gene Kelly was hired to do the Phils in 1950 and that's the year the Phils played in the World Series.

Kelly will be remembered for a call in a Phillies-Card game from St. Louis, which went into extra innings. It was about 1:30 A.M. Philadelphia time when Kelly described a ground out to shortstop, thusly, "...groundball to short, throw to first for the second out...and for those of you scoring in bed, that's 6-3."

There have been many imitators since, but Kelly was the first as far as I know.

Herb Carneal, the 1996 Ford Frick Award recipient who was my broadcast partner in Baltimore before moving to the Minnesota Twins in 1961, was involved in an amusing on-air exchange with Halsey Hall while doing a Twins' game.

An inning ended with a somewhat complicated rundown following a two-out hit into the left-field corner. The batter was out trying to stretch it into a double, with the center fielder finally making the tag after alertly coming in to cover second base.

After a commercial, Halsey asked for a recap of the scoring and as Herb ended with "...7-6-3-4-3-8," Halsey added wryly: "...and if a man answers, hang up."

That's enough sidetracking, let's go back to Byrum Saam, who, despite a distinguished career, missed the Phillies in the 1950 World Series. But when he retired 38 years in the business (1938-75), he went into the Broadcasters' Wing at Cooperstown.

Chapter 8

Working My Way Down

In the fall of 1948, I took advantage of a proferred expense-paid trip to Baltimore for a job interview by an ad agency representing the Gunther Brewing Co., one of the sponsors of Orioles baseball on the radio. In those days, Baltimore was an AAA minor league franchise.

At the office of the Ruthrauff and Ryan Advertising Agency on Hamilton Street, I met with Audrey Strauss and you might say I let it *all hang out* during our 30- to 40-minute conversation.

Let me explain. On the way back to the parking lot, while wondering if I had made an impression on Mrs. Strauss, I felt a cool breeze below my belt and soon learned to my great dismay that my pants fly had been open during the entire conversation.

I drove back to Philadelphia, convinced that I had seen the last of Baltimore because of my *faux pas*. But I was hired and I can't help but think that my on-air audition when I was pushed into the breach to replace the ailing Connie Desmond had played a part in their decision, the open fly notwithstanding.

After starting at the major league level of broadcasting, I was now doing International League games. As a stranger in a new city, the move was unsettling at first, and for the first year in Baltimore I was very unhappy.

It was so difficult getting my feet on the ground, I actually thought about going back to Philadelphia. But Quailey and Arthur told me to "hang in there," promising that things were going to get better...and, as usual, they were right.

When I had more time to think about my circumstances, I understood I should be happy just to have a job. I was just average at doing news broadcasts and while I did fairly well with record shows and ad-lib commercials, what I really wanted to do was play-by-play in football, baseball, basketball...all kinds of sports, and Baltimore would give me that opportunity.

In only my second or third Orioles broadcast, I saw O's infielder Ellis Clary climb the screen, jump in amongst the spectators, and start beating the daylights out of someone. I knew then that things were going to be a little different in Baltimore.

But one thing remained the same: I still didn't have to travel with the team. When the Orioles were on the road, I recreated games, with an operator at the road game relaying the play-by-play via Morse Code over the Western Union wire (a system later replaced by ticker tape).

My operator at the station was Ray Clampett, an avid baseball fan who was about as good as you could get. In recreated games, you stay about an inning behind the action early in the game to allow for rain delays or injuries, then in the seventh inning cut the lagtime down to a half inning.

Ray would type as he listened to the Morse Code, and hand me a piece of paper with the information I needed. Apparently some listeners were able to make sure bets because they understood the code they could hear ticking in the background and thus knew what would happen next. Later, the machines were enclosed to smother the sound.

By the ninth inning, we tried to be right on the pitch, and that's when Clampett's expertise was invaluable. Instead of writing the message, he employed hand signals.

For a strike, he'd hold up his right hand and go through the motions of a swing if the batter had swung, or make a "C" with his thumb and forefinger for a called strike. He used his left arm for a ball, using gestures to indicate if the pitch were high or low.

Working My Way Down

All I had to do was look at Ray and I could describe the action in my own fashion. When there was a foul ball, he'd make a swinging motion and point to indicate the direction of the foul. When the batter was retired, he'd cut the microphone and say, "grounded to short" or "flied to left."

The same thing for base hits: Cut the microphone and say, "single to left" or "double off the right-field wall." Recreations are a lot of fun to do, and it was really important then, because very few teams had broadcasters who traveled, particularly in the International League.

The system worked well for me because Ray made sure I didn't get into any trouble, but that didn't mean I couldn't create my own.

We were doing a game from Syracuse one night (I think it was in 1951), with the Orioles leading, 3-2, in the bottom of the ninth, two outs and the bases loaded, with Karl Drews pitching. The batter hit a flyball which left fielder Marv Rickert misjudged, and the O's lost the game.

But that wasn't the end of the story. When the game ended, I signed off and then spent about five minutes updating my statistics and getting the commercials in order for the next night, when the studio door opened and fellow staffer Gil Kriegel came in.

Gil shook his head and said, "How could that happen?"

I nodded in agreement and said: "Yeh, isn't that a nice way to get the *shit* kicked out of you?" Then, and only then, did I look up and see the red light was still on, meaning anybody still tuned in to the station could have heard me.

I learned later that Jack Dunn, the owner of the Orioles, had become so incensed over the outcome of the game that he threw his bedside radio through his bedroom window *(Ah, the power of a play-by-play broadcaster!)*.

Every now and then engineers, like broadcasters, make a mistake. Whoever the engineer was (I don't recall now), probably was in the process of transferring the power from one studio to another and just popped the wrong button at the same time I made my ill-timed remark.

Ain't the Beer Cold!

When I realized what had happened, I was truly sick...feeling the same way I did during my first week as a broadcaster when I cursed on the air in Reading. Coming to work the next day, I was hoping I could climb the stairs to the studio unseen.

But after I parked in a garage and started walking to WITH at 7 E. Lexington Street, I knew anonymity wasn't in the cards. I was barely out of the garage when the catcalls started and before I reached the station, four or five guys joined in the chorus, calling out things like, "Way to tell 'em, Chuck!" or "Helluva signoff, Thompson!"

I never got into too much trouble over that crude statement, but you don't forget things like that in broadcasting. It's happened to almost everyone in the business at one time or other...you think you're saying something and something else comes out. When dealing with the spoken word on a broadcast, you can't turn the pencil around and erase the mistake. When something is said, it's out there for all time.

Ernie Harwell, who preceded me into the Hall of Fame and was once my broadcast partner in Baltimore, tells a story about one of his own boo-boos. It happened while he was covering a Detroit Tigers game in California many years ago and there was a bang-bang play at the plate. Detroit catcher Bill Freehan made the tag and it appeared the runner was out, but the umpire gave the "safe" sign.

Freehan, naturally, was angry. Ernie, recapping the play for his listeners, said in all the years he had known Freehan, he had "never seen him quite so upset as he is now, standing at homeplate *beating his meat...mitt.*"

Ernie recovered quickly in an attempt to cover his mistake, but not quite soon enough to prevent the misspeak. But those kinds of things do happen in the wonderful world of play-by-play, even to a Hall-of-Famer like Ernie.

Getting back to Rickert, I was told some stories about Marv when he played with the Boston Braves (who later became the Milwaukee Braves and, eventually, the Atlanta Braves).

One day, during a game in Boston, Marv kept telling the

Working My Way Down

umpires that it was too cold to play. When that didn't elicit any sympathy, he gathered some paper cups and newspapers, and lit a fire in the dugout. The game continued, but Marv was excused from further action.

Another time, during a persistent rain, Marv asked everytime he was in the vicinity of the first base umpire, "How long are you doing to let us play in this mess?" Again, he got no response.

So, in one inning, Marv headed for the outfield carrying two or three towels, which he spread on the field in his position and stepped atop them. The result was the same: the game went on without Marv.

I was near the cage one day while the International League Orioles were taking batting practice, when Marv walked up and asked if he could take a drag off my cigarette. He must have had a hard night because he looked as though he was suffering from a hangover.

I refused, figuring Marv may get into trouble for smoking on the field. But he persisted and put things into perspective when he said, "You have to learn how to handicap yourself...never come out here feeling too strong."

In the fall of 1949, I started doing play-by-play of Navy football and also for the Colts in the All-America Conference, in which the Colts played before the league disbanded and they came back to town as a National Football League club.

I went to Chicago to do a Colts' game at venerable Soldier Field with veteran broadcaster Bill Dyer doing the color. I had never worked alongside Bill, who had a great reputation in Baltimore, so I didn't know what to expect. I soon found out.

The Colts, then coached by Cecil Isbell, couldn't seem to get into the game in the first half and dropped a lot of passes. That kind of nettled my broadcast partner.

When I turned the microphone over to Bill, I intended to stay and have a conversation about the first half. But I didn't have a chance to interrupt what turned out to be a lengthy monologue which bordered on a soliloquy.

I didn't know where he was headed at the outset and I can't

recall his remarks verbatim. But with great emotion, Bill lamented the fact that with all the great medical minds in Baltimore, at Johns Hopkins Hospital and other facilities, recognized worldwide, that no one had been able to develop a serum that could be innoculated into football players so they they might hold onto the ball.

Bill was familiar with his audience and apparently knew how far he could go with that approach. But the whole concept didn't make any sense to me; it was kind of off the wall and slightly embarrassing. So I got up and left the booth without commenting. At the time, I didn't understand Dyer's sense of humor or his reading of the Baltimore listeners' psyche.

When I was doing baseball and things weren't going well for the Orioles, fans would suggest that I walk around a little red chair to change the team's luck. That didn't make any sense either, but I was told that's the way Bill used to get a rally started.

Then I found out the rally voodoo was used only in recreated games, when he knew from the telegraphic messages that the Orioles were going to score. The little red chair might by synonymous with my "Ain't the beer cold!" and "Go to war, Miss Agnes," except my pet phrases were used after the fact and Dyer was doing his schtick when he was certain something good for the home team was going to happen.

Although Dyer was taking advantage of the listening audience, that was the way he chose to do his promoting and it worked splendidly. No one did more to promote sports in Baltimore than Bill Dyer, but his method was a bit unsettling for me.

The little red chair was quite a gimmick, like Harry Caray singing "Take Me Out to the Ballgame" in Chicago, or Bob Prince waving a salami in Pittsburgh to stir up the fans.

Before Prince, there was Rosey Rosewell, who did a lot of wonderful things with sound effects while recreating Pirates games on the air. When he knew a home run was coming, he'd say, "Open the window, Aunt Minnie, here she comes!" and then drop a tray of broken dishes and other dinnerware.

I never believed in sound effects and in my wildest imagination, I couldn't have come up with the idea of walking around the chair for luck. If I had done that in Philadelphia, I'd probably have ended up in New Jersey.

In addition to my sports broadcasting, I did some record shows in Baltimore at WITH and WCBM. At WITH, where I was hired by Jake Embry, I worked with Gil Kriegel, Hot Rod Hulbert, Lee Case, Howard Rudolph, Hugh Wanke, and Buddy Dean, who later achieved fame with the afternoon record hop for teenagers on WJZ-TV. They were all well-known radio personalities in Baltimore at the time, and were a great bunch to work alongside.

At WITH, I spun records from 1 P.M. until 6 o'clock, and I started one thing that seemed to have an impact on the city; at least, it generated a lot of phone calls.

Every Saturday for three of the five hours I was on the air, I presented the music of one band. The first to be featured was the *Glen Miller Anniversary Album*, which I played in its entirety.

That got me started, and I followed in subsequent weeks with Benny Goodman, Count Basie, or singers such as Frank Sinatra or Ella Fitzgerald. And to add to the enjoyment, there were few commercials on Saturdays to interrupt the melodies.

Radio stations around the city would call, asking what I would be featuring on the next show. For me, it was a heck of a thing to play the kind of music I liked so much and it didn't hurt to have such an enthusiastic audience.

I also worked on WCBM, which had a popular late-night record show hosted by Harley Brinsfield, who served on the State Roads Commission and also started the Harley's Sub Shop around town.

Harley's show, which featured jazz and some "hep" comments from the host, was on one night when station newsman Charles Roeder called in from the Maryland Penitentiary to report on the execution of G. Edward Grammer, who had been convicted of killing his wife.

After the report from Roeder, Harley returned to the microphone and said matter-of-factly: "Man, there's one cat that ain't digging me tonight."

My memories of the major league Orioles have kind of

overshadowed those from the International League days, but some incidents keep coming out of my memory bank from my first few years in Baltimore.

First and foremost, I recall that the layout of the diamond in Municipal Stadium was a lot different than it was when the O's returned to the American League in 1954.

When I first started covering the team in 1949, homeplate was located in what later became left field and it was just 270 feet down the left-field line. Howie Moss hit a mess of homers to left field, as he did for Baltimore's glorious 1944 Little World Series champions, but by 1949 he was no longer playing for the Orioles.

The right-field side was wide open, extending out toward 33rd Street, with Eastern High School in the background. The only thing to stop a ball hit that way was the Administration Building, some 600 or more feet away.

By the time homeplate was moved to where it was later, the Orioles were a pretty good team, but when I came to town they were just average, under manager Tommy Thomas.

In 1950, center fielder Butch Woyt probably had to work harder for his paycheck than anyone in baseball, strictly because of his mates in the outfield. In right was Babe Barna, who had played briefly for the Philadelphia A's, New York Giants, and Red Sox in the late '30s and early '40s and was, by that time, over the hill and could hardly move. Anse Moore, who had played 51 games with the Detroit Tigers in 1946, had much the same problem in left field. So balls hit into either gap belonged to Butch; he had no choice. Barna's and Moore's favorite expression had to be: "You got it."

In the 1950 playoffs against Montreal, I remember another bases loaded situation, and again with Karl Drews pitching for the O's. This time, he threw wildly past the plate and catcher Clyde Kluttz. Kluttz tore off his mask and turned to chase the ball, only to find it coming back to him after hitting the backstop. The runners couldn't advance and Drews got out of the inning.

The caliber of ball in the International League was a notch below what I had been seeing in Philadelphia, but a lot of the players

Working My Way Down

eventually made it to the big leagues. Some of the names I ran across still intrigue me. Like Carden Gillenwater and Estel Crabtree, both of whom were back after having played in the majors.

One of the main differences was the caliber of broadcast facilities, some of which were just plain laughable. When we barnstormed north from spring training, we stopped at some charming southern towns with less-than-appealing accommodations for the broadcasters.

At one stop, we broadcast from ground level, only 10 to 15 feet behind homeplate. At another place, I watched the action by peeking through an aperture in the right-field scoreboard where they hung the scores. But it was the game that counted, not the ease of doing the job.

Just about everywhere you go these days, even in the minors, most of the facilities for radio and television are pretty good.

Nick Cullop, nicknamed "Tomato Puss" because of his red features, was the manager in 1950, and we went to spring training in Hollywood, Florida. There was an exhibition game scheduled in Havana, Cuba, but I didn't go because the game was not to be broadcast.

Pitcher Irv Medlinger was from the Chicago area and apparently had never been near the Atlantic Ocean. He didn't like to fly and when he heard the team was going to Havana, he asked Cullop if it would be all right if he didn't take a plane. Cullop, thinking Medlinger was going to go by boat, said OK, only to have Medlinger ask, "Which road do I take?"

The O's infield in 1950 had George Byam at first, Bobby Young at second, Eddie Pellagrini at short, and Russ Kerns at third.

Young, a native of Granite, Maryland, near BWI Airport in Baltimore County, later played for the major league Orioles after the American League franchise in St. Louis was moved to Baltimore.

I recall a game in Fenway Park when Boston pitchers knocked him down twice with inside pitches and the competitive Young took revenge in the best way possible. With Ted Williams on first base, the shortstop fielded a grounder and tossed to Young for the forceout of Williams. Young stepped on the bag and made his relay throw from down around his knees, causing Ted to go down in 17 pieces while trying to avoid the ball.

The Red Sox never threw at Young again, convincing me that that was the best way to handle the situation rather than throwing the bat or running out to the mound to attack the pitcher.

Pellagrini was the first player I ever saw to wear uniform No. 13, a number that no one wanted in those days because of the bad luck connotations. It was used sparingly in subsequent years, and one of the first was pitcher Steve Barber, the first 20-game winner for the Orioles in the major leagues.

But nowadays, No. 13 is no longer rare. While reporting on games in 1995, I can recall seeing the number on Lance Parrish, Ozzie Guillen, Jim Leyritz, Omar Vizquel, Brent Gates, and Mike Pagliarulo, and there may have been others.

One of the highlights of covering the Orioles was associating with Eddie Weidner, a one-of-a-kind character who started as a scoreboard operator for the minor league Orioles in 1916 at the age of 14 and stayed until his retirement in 1967 after working more than 40 years as a trainer.

Fond memories of Eddie's way of doing things or his home-spun bon mots still bring a smile to my face.

I was sitting on a hotel porch with Eddie in Florida one evening, and we had nothing better to do than exercise the rocking chairs. There was an extended period of silence before Eddie said, "Look at that."

I figured he meant the moon and responded, "Yeh, that's about as beautiful as a moon can get."

"No, no."

Well, it wasn't the moon, so I tried another approach: "Look at that big honker of a pelican out there...look at the size of him."

"No," Eddie said again. "Look at that tide."

"What about it?"

"The tide rolls in and the tide rolls out...then what have you got?" I was still chuckling when I went to bed that night.

During the regular season, a young pitcher was pulled from the mound after giving up a home-run ball and Eddie went to the clubhouse to ice him down. The kid was in a snit, throwing chairs and just having a terrible time. He threw another chair and yelled, "That S.O.B. will never get a pitch like that from me again. I've got a memory like an elephant!"

Again, Eddie had his own special rejoinder: "What's an elephant got to remember?"

In the minors in those days, Eddie didn't have the ethel chloride spray which is used nowadays to numb the pain of injuries. He still used the cheaper remedy—ice—to reduce the swelling. One Sunday morning in Montreal, he went to a drugstore for some ice and struck up a conversation with a guy standing in line who happened to be a doctor. The doc asked Eddie if he had ever tried ethyl chloride and the Orioles' trainer said he had never even heard of it.

Eddie was impressed and when he said he would have to try some, the doctor volunteered to write him a prescription.

"I tried it," Eddie said. "I think it cost $3.50."

How did it work?

"Let's put it this way...I couldn't have carried $3.50 worth of ice."

Eddie was simply a nice person to be around and one night in Arizona, my broadcast partner Bailey Goss and I asked him to accompany us to dinner. "Bails" and I always had a couple of cocktails before dinner. Eddie didn't drink alcohol, but he'd drink as much coffee as the waiter could pour. We informed the maitre d' and Eddie didn't diappoint us. He must have had a gallon or more of coffee during the meal.

When the Orioles returned to the American League in 1954, the club made a wise decision in taking both Eddie and Jack Dunn, who became the traveling secretary, with them. The move was made after the St. Louis Browns franchise was purchased for $2,475,000 (compare that with the $173 million paid by Peter Angelos when he bought the Orioles in 1993).

Permit me to do a little backtracking here. After covering the International League Orioles for three years, I was fired by Gunther after the 1951 season. The brewery didn't think it needed

Ain't the Beer Cold!

a salaried play-by-play announcer and, in those days, and I guess they didn't.

But there were no hard feelings, especially after Jake Embry hired me to do music and sports shows on WITH and, more importantly, continue to broadcast Orioles home games and recreated road games—an assignment that I continued through the 1953 season.

Chapter 9

Back to the Major Leagues

The people of Baltimore went bonkers when it was announced on September 29, 1953, that the city was coming back to the major leagues for the first time since 1902. But not me—I was told that I couldn't be an Orioles' broadcaster.

The National Brewing Co. was to be the major Orioles sponsor and I was disqualified because of my previous connections with the Gunther Brewing Co.

Gunther had brought me to Baltimore in 1949 and my name was by this time associated with their products. I had grown to like Baltimore and some of the city seemed to like me, so sitting out the 1954 season was one of my more difficult times. I wasn't angry over that decision but, to say the least, I was upset and maybe felt sorry for myself at being left out of the city's return to Major League Baseball.

Looking over some of the mementoes from my career recently, I came across a letter I had sent to my parents on November 29, 1953, written on WITH stationary. In it I tried to explain my dilemma. I pointed out I had worked for the Gunther Brewing Co. and for American Beer, and was now trying to get a job with the National Brewing Co.

"In other words," I wrote, "two seasons ago I told everybody

Ain't the Beer Cold!

that Gunther was the best beer in the world, last year I told them American was the best and this year I want the chance to tell them that National is the best." I told Mom and Dad it was tough to make the brewery people understand "that the job of a play-by-play baseball announcer is to sell baseball and not just the product that sponsors the games.

"Actually and factually, I know that the color man's job is to sell the product and the play-by-play man the game, but you try and make them see it."

It was made more frustrating because the ballclub and the fans wanted me to do the games and so did Bailey Goss, who was the color man and an old friend from my radio days in Reading.

But eventually, things began to break my way. During my years in Baltimore, I had developed a friendship with Norman Almony and Pat Roche of the National Brewing Co. Late in the 1954 baseball season, I think it was in August, Norman called and invited me to lunch with both of them.

At lunch, I was told they wanted me to meet Jerry Hoffberger, the boss at National. So we went right to the brewery and I met Jerry for the first time. During a conversation of about 20 to 25 minutes, I was told National wanted me to be part of the play-by-play Orioles' coverage.

At the end of the brief meeting, we didn't sign a contract. Jerry and I merely shook hands to seal the deal, and that handshake lasted 23 years.

That handshake got me back into Major League Baseball and I was also able to continue my National Football League coverage. It was one of the greatest single events of my life and I'm proud to say that to this day Jerry is still a good friend.

Jerry also suggested a change in my on-camera appearance after he saw me standing hatless during a network telecast from Baltimore's Memorial Stadium as I conducted an interview during a National Football League game.

Jerry, who had seen the telecast in California, called his office the next day and said, "Tell that son-of-a-gun to put a hat on." He was paying the bills, so from then on, I wore a lid on my bald head when I was on camera.

94

Back to the Major Leagues

I covered the Orioles with Ernie Harwell in 1955 and 1956, at a time when the team was struggling to improve on the record of its predecessors, the St. Louis Browns.

In 52 years, the Browns had won only one pennant (the war year of 1944) and had finished in the first division only one more time (11) than it had been in last place (10). They were last in the eight-team league in 1953, and 18 players from the Browns were still with the Orioles in 1954.

While the 54-100 record of the Orioles in their inaugural season matched that of the Browns the year before, the O's moved up to seventh place ahead of Philadelphia. But they were still a whopping 57 games behind pennant-winning Cleveland.

Paul Richards took over as general manager late in 1954 and also replaced Jimmy Dykes as field manager the following season. Richards made bold moves right from the start, engineering a 17-player trade with the New York Yankees in November 1954, one of the biggest in baseball history.

An ambidextrous pitcher during his high school days, Richards was also adept at dishing out bonus money with both hands as he signed young players throughout the country.

Richards was criticized for his spending habits as he slowly built the team, but he snatched at least one gem at bargain-basement prices. Brooks Robinson was signed for a $4,000 bonus before launching his Hall-of-Fame career.

The 1955 season was marked by Orioles player shuffling. Richards used 54 players that year, 10 at third base alone. Only three times did the same players start and finish a game.

Some newspaper guys in those days occasionally would complain about Richards and I found that hard to believe because I got to be a friend of the *tall, taciturn Texan* (as he was known in print). I respected Paul as a manager and played a lot of golf with him. On the links we didn't talk baseball, it was all golf.

As a play-by-play broadcaster, I had no special need for any inside information. A newspaperman may think it's an advantage to know something others aren't aware of, but I didn't think that would help me.

Ain't the Beer Cold!

My job is to tell the listeners what happened on the field, not why; who hit the ball and where it went, the number of outs, the inning, and the score. The whys of what happened, I think, are for the newspapermen. After the game, the writers can go to the clubhouse and find out why so-and-so failed to cover the base. My job was just to tell what happened on the field.

I remember a trip to Chicago in May 1956, when the Orioles acquired future Hall-of-Famer George Kell to play third base. Bailey Goss and I used to kill time on the road playing pool, and on this night we went out with second baseman Billy Gardner and writer Hugh Trader of the *Baltimore News-Post*. Gardner was nicknamed "The Sniper" and one had only to look at how much production he engendered from a low batting average to realize the derivation of the moniker. Billy would be hitting .230 and all of a sudden he'd come up with a double to win the game.

Billy was also adept at playing pool, maybe even somewhat of a shark, and it was he who suggested we go run a few racks. None of us had any extra cash, so I called Richards on the phone, went to his suite, and negotiated a $100 loan.

As I moved to leave the room, Paul said, "You know this guy, don't you?" I looked and there was Kell.

"How are you, George," I said, shook hands and hustled out to grab a cab for the pool hall.

Gardner didn't stay with us very long because he had his eyes on a game at the other end of the room where there was a little money involved. He was looking for a stake and I told him all I had was what I borrowed from Richards. He asked for half and I gave him $50.

At about 11 o'clock or so, I said to Bailey, "You know who was up in Paul's room—George Kell."

"What? Who?" Trader barked. "You dumb S.O.B." With that, he threw down his cue stick, grabbed his coat, and out he went. Hugh was really angry because I hadn't told about Kell being with Richards earlier in the evening.

Hell, I didn't know that the Orioles had traded pitcher Jim Wilson and outfielder Dave Philley to the White Sox for Kell and

Back to the Major Leagues

pitchers Mike Fornieles and Connie Johnson. What's more, I didn't really care at that moment. I'm just a play-by-play guy. All I know is "ball one, strike two—" and I was off-duty.

Hugh was a real bulldog because he was so tenacious. If he got hold of a story, you couldn't shake him. He would call Richards, no matter what the hour of the day, and Paul was the kind of a person who would go to bed about 9:30.

When we trained in Arizona in 1956, Richards decided to visit his home in Waxahachie, Texas, on the day off before an exhibition game in Los Angeles. He was to leave at 4:30 A.M. to travel by rail, since he didn't like to fly.

With his bags ready, Paul went to the lobby, and the last thing he did was to telephone Trader to ask if he needed to know anything before he left. He didn't want to be tracked down at home, I presume.

Richards was a very intelligent guy with a good sense of humor. He knew how to take advantage of an opponents' mistakes and if there was a loophole in the baseball regulations, he was quick to take advantage if he thought it would help his team.

Paul came up with the oversized mitt so his catchers could handle Hoyt Wilhelm's knuckleball. The pillow-sized glove was later reduced in size by a new regulation from the rules committee, but Paul had gotten around the previous rule until it was changed.

Paul worked on another idea that didn't pan out as well. It was his contention that catchers sometimes had difficulty handling throws from the outfield because their mitts weren't flexible enough to provide enough dexterity.

So Paul suggested that when a pitcher ran behind the plate to back up a throw from the outfield, the pitcher and catcher should exchange gloves as they passed one another.

That certainly sounded innovative, and Paul was anxious to give it a try at the earliest opportunity. So, the Orioles decided to experiment in an exhibition game.

Sure enough, the play came up and the exchange was made. There was one major problem—the pitcher involved was a lefthander, and the catcher couldn't get the glove on his hand to make the catch. No rule change was necessary to end that idea.

Under Paul, the Orioles were extremely well schooled. It was Paul who laid the foundation of major league baseball in Baltimore and for 30 years (1957 through 1986) the team had the best winning percentage in the game, a Paul Richards' legacy.

Before I started covering the Orioles, I was told that umpire Eddie Rommel, a former major league pitcher who lived near Memorial Stadium, had saved the city a lot of expense and embarrassment.

Eddie wandered into the park one day to visit with general manager Art Ehlers as surveyors and a construction crew were about to erect the scoreboard in dead center field. Rommel knew better, pointing out that the location would force batters to look into the scoreboard lights while trying to track the pitches.

After Eddie alerted Ehlers, plans were changed and the scoreboard was erected in right-center field. That was one umpire's decision that couldn't be disputed.

Rommel was once involved in a classic confrontation with pitcher Billy Loes, who played for the O's from 1956 to 1959 after achieving fame with the Brooklyn Dodgers.

Some of the off-the-wall antics of Loes didn't sit well with Rommel, a member of the old school who took his job and the game rather seriously.

Loes complained one night that Rommel was squeezing the strike zone on him during a game at Memorial Stadium. The pitcher stared Rommel's way after a ball was called, but never said a word. After another called ball, Loes indicated his disgust by tossing his glove in the air.

Another pitch, and another ball. Loes left the mound and started toward the plate. One could almost read Rommel's mind—this is just what he wanted Loes to do. So the umpire stepped around the catcher and waited with hands on his hips.

But Loes, moving swiftly, never looked at Rommel and simply went around the arbiter to begin a conversation with the

Back to the Major Leagues

catcher! Rommel was left high and dry in front of the plate and all he could do was turn around and sweep the plate clean.

Umpire John Stevens, who lived in Philadelphia, liked to work games in Baltimore because he loved crabcakes.

He was working a game while construction was still being done on Memorial Stadium, and there was a metal sign in foul territory of the right-field lower deck, listing the name of the contractor.

Dick Stuart of Boston, a right-handed batter, hit a ball off the end of the bat down the right-field line. Stevens, the ump at first base, turned and watched the flight of the ball. He had no sooner gotten his arm in the air to indicate a home run, when the ball went "BANG" off the metal sign.

Stuart jumped high in the air and galloped around the bases, clapping his hands in delight. After the game, I visited the umpires' room. There was John Stevens, looking a little peaked as he sipped a beer.

I asked what happened and John, shaking his head, said: "Charley, all I can tell you, the last time I *seen* that damned thing, it was fair." That was good enough for me.

When I first covered the Orioles at Memorial Stadium, I always noted a group of guys, maybe 20 or so, near the edge of the stadium on the third-base side. They never bothered anyone and nobody bothered them.

It took a little while before I realized they were gamblers who bet on everything imaginable, even on the next pitch. I'd never seen that before, but it didn't bother me. I figure if a guy wants to waste his money, or make money that way, it's his own privilege.

When I covered the Senators in the late 1950s, my broadcast partner Bob Wolff (who joined me in the Hall of Fame in 1995) and I were obligated to attend the annual Baseball Writers' dinner in New York. One year, the veteran Washington beat writers, like Shirley Povich, Morrie Siegel, Francis Stann, and Bob Addie— all pretty good elbow-benders—told me they would cut out of the banquet early and head for Toots Shor's restaurant to tell a few lies, laugh it up, and have a few drinks.

Ain't the Beer Cold!

Jerry Hoffberger was the host of our party, and so about 10:30 P.M. or so I apologized to him and said I was headed for bed. "OK, kid, take care of yourself," Jerry said. But instead of going back to the hotel, I joined the rest of the guys and headed for Toots' upscale bar. We were there about 45 minutes, having a heck of a good time, talking baseball and nonsense, and having arguments, when someone tapped me on the shoulders. I turned around—and there was Jerry Hoffberger.

He started to laugh and then said, "Kid, you've got one helluva bedroom." Then he bought the next round and was happy to stay with us for the remainder of a wonderful evening.

Two of the great drinkers I've known in my time were Toots Shor and comedian Jackie Gleason, both of them big guys of tremendous girth.

One night Jack said he could walk around the block in Manhattan faster than Toots, but was challenged and they wound up betting $100 on the outcome. They went outside, took off in opposite directions, and the rest of us went back inside the bar to await the outcome.

Within two minutes, in comes an unruffled Jack. He sits at the bar, orders another drink, and about five minutes later here comes a huffing-and-puffing Toots.

Jack later revealed he had walked around the corner and jumped into a cab to facilitate his trip. Toots accused him of all sorts of crimes against humanity—but he paid off the bet.

Visiting teams who came into Washington's old Griffith Stadium used to complain quite regularly about the hymns being played on a carillon by a church across the street on Florida Avenue. The music, they said, lulled them to sleep rather than pepped them up for batting practice.

During my tenure in Washington, I also did NBC-TV's "Game of the Week" and was on the network to call the 1960 World Series between the New York Yankees and Pittsburgh Pirates.

The World Series was especially weird that year. The Yanks outscored the Pirates, 55-27, winning by scores of 16-3 in Game 2, 10-0 in Game 3, and 12-0 in Game 6. But the Pirates won the Series, taking the seventh and deciding game, 10-9.

Back to the Major Leagues

Baseball fans will remember the bad-hop grounder which struck New York shortstop Tony Kubek in the throat and led to five Pittsburgh runs in the eighth, the two Yankee runs which tied the score in the ninth, and Bill Mazeroski's game-winning homer in the bottom of the ninth.

But I have my own special memory of the climatic ninth, the only World Series game decided on a sudden-death homer until Joe Carter of Toronto homered in the ninth inning of Game 6 to beat Philadelphia, 8-6, in the final game of the 1993 Fall Classic.

I called Mazeroski's homer on radio and, for some unknown reason, gave the final score as 10-0 instead of 10-9. Not only that, I told the listening audience that the homer had been hit off Art Ditmar instead of Ralph Terry. I think I had just seen Ditmar warming up in the bullpen.

That was easily the most embarrassing moment of my career behind the microphone. But when Pirates' broadcaster Bob Prince called me during the off-season and asked if I'd like to redo the ending for a souvenir record the Pirates were going to produce, I declined. I figured it had gone on the air that way, so it wouldn't be honest to change it. But I must admit, I'd done nothing quite so embarrassing before, or since.

Chapter 10

My Introduction to the NFL

My introduction to pro football in Baltimore had a sputtering start, mainly because that's the same way the franchises were going at the time.

The Colts were members of the ill-fated All-America Conference from 1947 through 1949, and then joined the National Football League for the 1950 season before owner Abe Watner tossed in the towel after one season. They resurfaced in 1953, laying the groundwork for one of the NFL's best teams.

Watner sold the franchise back to the league after suffering significant losses in 1950. I learned from the players that the boss once had counted *sticks of gum* so that each would receive only one per game.

His losses included a wad of paper money that blew out of an open window of his office on Baltimore Street due either to a gust of wind or an office fan. Watner told me that only a small part of the $10,000 that was in the stack was blown out, but it was enough to cause passers-by to scramble on the sidewalk for $100 bills.

Watner was a very quiet gentleman whose knowledge of football was strictly as a fan. But he surprised me in a lot of ways, one of which was acquiring eight players from the Chicago Bears in a trade for offensive guard Dick Barwegen. Apparently, Abe's wife convinced Abe than anytime you can get eight for one, it was a good deal.

I recall that when we traveled to Los Angeles to play the Rams, Abe said that in his dream the Colts had won, 21-7. Everyone merely smiled, but then all agreed that wouldn't it be nice if the dream came true.

Well, Abe almost had the correct score. The Colts did score the 21—but the Rams wound up with 70. As Abe reasoned, maybe the Good Lord forgot to tell him about the zero behind the "7."

After two years without a team after the Watner era ended, the Colts rejoined the NFL in 1953 by satisfying a league requirement to sell 15,000 season tickets. That was a great story in those days because the ticket buyers didn't know their seat locations, or even which team would be coming to Baltimore, before putting their money on the line.

The people of Baltimore wanted a football team and expressed themselves in the best way they knew how. Thus began one of the great eras in the history of the NFL as the Colts went on to become one of the most respected teams ever.

Buddy Young, a short and slashing runner, was a standout of those early Colt teams and an inspiration to his teammates because of the great heart he exhibited playing against oversized competition.

Ironically, Buddy died of a heart attack some years after he retired while driving from a funeral, and it still hurts when I think of that incident. Whenever Buddy's name comes up in conversation, he's still remembered with affection.

I'll never forget the memorial service for Buddy—a heartbreaking day for all of us. Art Donovan spoke and, with tears running down his cheaks, told of his love for his departed teammate and concluded with, "I'll tell you another thing, he's the only S.O.B. that could ever get me to wear a necktie." The church service didn't intimidate old Artie.

One of the great rejoinders in the history of pro sports is attributed to Donovan, although he might deny it. One day at the Colts' training camp in Westminster, Maryland, one of the team's early draft picks—an offensive tackle from Ohio State—was being tutored on pass blocking. As you may know, Coach Woody Hayes had a run-oriented offense at Ohio State and said the only passing he wanted from his Buckeyes was in the classroom. So, there was much to be done.

Anyway, the youngster was pitted in the drill against Hall-of-Famer Gino Marchetti, the best pass rusher of his day and maybe the best of all time. Gino feinted and got past the kid twice, and on the third effort he punctuated the mismatch by leapfrogging over the dazzled rookie.

Totally frustrated, the kid turned to John Sandusky and asked the offensive line coach, "What do I do now?" Donovan, who was looking on, had the perfect answer when he deadpanned: "Applaud!"

Donovan, a massive defensive tackle, and Buddy were roommates at the Colts' training camp in Westminster, Maryland, and they were a combo to behold. Artie was an inveterate needler, and Buddy loved every minute of the verbal abuse.

As you know, Artie was a light eater (from dawn till dusk) and Buddy came into the room one night to find Artie in bed with nothing on the TV except the test pattern. Buddy went over to turn the set off when he heard:

"Don't touch that, you little S.O.B. It's keeping my pizza warm!"

We were in Los Angeles for a game one season when Buddy slipped on some steps outside the hotel and was knocked out. I was one of about five or six in the group that was somewhat panic stricken. One guy ran into the hotel to ask for an ambulance and another went looking for a policeman. Finally, we got the help we needed and Buddy recovered.

John Steadman, covering the game for the *Baltimore News-Post*, had written several columns defending a Colts' fan who bothered some of the spectators back home by blowing a bugle in the stadium on 33rd Street. John backed up his words by bringing the bugle on the roadtrip and had it with him when Buddy fell.

Asked why he hadn't blown the bugle out on the street, John

said, "If I did as Buddy was coming to, he might think it was the angel Gabriel."

Another Colts player with the same kind of class as Buddy Young was wide receiver Raymond Berry. Slightly built and not swift afoot, Raymond was picked by the Colts on the 20th round of the 1954 draft as a "future" because he still had a year of college eligibility left.

Raymond joined the team the following year and made up for his physical shortcomings with tedious hours of extra practice and by paying painstaking attention to the minutest of details. He made the Hall of Fame the hard way, he *earned* it. Raymond was the first player I ever saw who used netting under the goalposts as he practiced catching passes, to stop errant or misjudged balls so that they wouldn't have to be chased. And no one spent more time looking at film than Berry

When we were going to California for a game, Raymond would live on West Coast time for a week, changing his mealtimes and bedtimes to prepare his body for the three-hour time difference.

For games at Kezar Stadium in San Franciso, Raymond knew he could be looking into a setting sun while trying to track John Unitas' passes in the second half. So he wore sunglasses when the Colts were moving from west to east on the field, and Raymond may have been a pioneer in playing the sunfield in football.

There was nothing fancy about Raymond's lifestyle. I recall a night in San Francisco, after the Colts had clinched the division title and we were celebrating in general manager Don Kellett's suite. I happened to look out of a window at a big fruit stand across the street and there were Raymond and linebacker Don Shinnick leaving the stand carrying huge bags of fruit. They went to their rooms, propped up their feet and gorged themselves on fruit while other players were anticipating a night of steaks and beer.

The Los Angeles Coliseum posed some problems for broadcasters. It was so huge that the players looked about a foot high from the broadcast booth, making identifications difficult. Conditions improved with the advent of television, when even radio broadcasters were able to follow the action on the TV monitors.

The toughest working conditions I ever encountered at a football game were in Foxboro, Massachusetts, where the Colts were playing the Patriots. The booth had a fixed window that couldn't be opened, and that was fine because it kept the booth warm during those freezing New England winters.

But cold weather wasn't the problem for this particular radio broadcast of a Monday Night "Game of the Week." It rained in torrents and it was hard to see through the closed window. Next time you're driving in a rainstorm, turn off the windshield wipers for a few moments and you'll know what I mean.

Back to the Coliseum—that's where I got a personal insight into the character of Colts quarterback John Unitas and what made him one of the special players of all time.

The Colts had been beaten by the Rams that day and eliminated from championship consideration. The locker room silence was eerie. After such defeats, you try to avoid eye contact with anyone because you know they are hurting.

I was leaning against a wall with my head down, not looking at anyone. All of a sudden I felt a finger beneath my nose (actually, there's room under my nose for more than one finger), my head was lifted up and there I was, looking into Unitas'eyes.

John never said a word as he continued on into the shower. But that brief encounter told me a lot about the man: No matter how badly it hurts, you can't take it with you, so just get ready for the next game.

Most professional athletes I've known, particularly in football where they play only once a week, have that kind of attitude. Some did let losses disrupt their lives at home, but, to my knowledge, John never took the game home with him. He hated losing as much as any man in the world, but he wasn't going to think about it any longer. All he could do was get ready for the next game.

Another look into the Unitas psyche occurred many years later, when we both attended a charity function for The Cystic Fibrosis Foundation. John and I had our conversation interrupted

My Introduction to the NFL

by a New York Giants' fan who looked into the old quarterback's eyes and said, "Unitas, I've hated your guts all my life—in 1958 when I was 10 years old, you broke my heart (referring to the Colts' victory over the Giants in the overtime championship game)."

John looked at me and smiled, then turned back to the gentleman and said quietly, yet forcefully: "Believe me, sir, it was my pleasure."

One of the most gifted of all Colts was running back Lenny Moore, who could do it all—zigzag like a scared jack rabbit through the opposition and catch passes like a wide receiver.

There would be many things to remember in my record of Lenny Moore highlights, but the one that would rank among the best would be the time he scored against Green Bay when seven different Packers had a shot at him from 15 yards out and couldn't knock him down.

I also recall Lenny catching a pass in the late moments of a game in Kezar Stadium, giving the Colts a victory over the San Francisco 49ers. After the game, there was hardly room to move in the locker room as the media sought quotes from both Lenny and John Unitas.

I only heard part of one conversation when someone asked Lenny what the play was that produced the TD.

"Man, I'm way out there and with all the noise, I didn't have any idea what the play was," Lenny said. "I just took off and, fortunately, John read me." Just two old pros at work.

Practice sessions for the Colts were sometimes just as tough as the games on Sunday. The media was allowed on the field at Memorial Stadium, standing behind either the offensive huddle or the defensive huddle, and you had to be alert to avoid being trampled.

Defensive day was on Thursday, when the Colts were tested by the plays of the upcoming opponent. Alex Hawkins usually played the part of the opposition's running back, an assignment he didn't relish. He just wanted to play the regular game, so one Thursday he was just going through the motions.

Alex just jogged on the plays, almost in slow motion, instead of testing the defense with plays that developed quickly.

Ain't the Beer Cold!

Defensive back Bobby Boyd had seen enough. He came up from the corner and belted the Hawk pretty good. As Alex was on his hands and knees trying to clear his head, everybody on defense began to bark like dogs. The message had been delivered, loud and clear.

Hawkins was one of the more delightful, engaging personalities of the Colts. He was an outstanding player but he definitely marched to a different drummer. Not all the rules of the game appealed to him.

That was evident even in college. Marvin Bass, his coach at the University of South Carolina, told me that a thunderstorm developed at practice one day and the players ran for the locker room as lightning flashed all around.

Everybody, that is, except Alex. When teammates yelled for him to hurry and join the others in the safety of cover, Alex reassured the other Gamecocks: "Don't worry, it's me He's after."

Alex had various ways of getting into trouble, none more unusual than the time he decided to avoid curfew the night before a road game by climbing down the outside of the hotel to set himself free of restraint.

He reasoned that if he went out through the lobby, he would be spotted by the coaches. Instead, he exited the elevator at the mezzanine level and went through a window while heading for a big pile of sand left by a construction crew. But Alex's "human fly" performance attracted some spectators, one of whom was line coach John Sandusky. As soon as the Hawk hit the sidewalk, Sandusky greeted him with: "Weeb wants to see you."

So, it was up to Weeb Ewbank's suite, where the head coach lectured on the responsibility to family, teammates, the game of football, and even to Weeb himself. "Plus that," Weeb finished, "you now owe me $500."

Alex peeled the money off his roll of bills, put the money on Weeb's desk, and said, "Coach, if you're going to dance, you've got to pay the fiddler."

Then Hawkins disappeared, but instead of going to his room, he went far out into the night. He showed up the next day and played a good game.

My Introduction to the NFL

Alex also was the focal point of an incident one night at the Golden Arm Restaurant in the Towson area, then owned by Unitas and Bobby Boyd.

After the bar closed, everyone stayed around swapping stories and finishing their drinks. Finally, Alex got up to leave, but Boyd said, "You're not going anywhere. For all those nights on the road that you kept me out after curfew, tonight I'm getting even." The guy who opened the Golden Arm the next morning found the Hawk asleep on the floor.

As captain of the Colts' special team, Hawkins would join offensive captain Unitas and defensive captain Gino Marchetti in the center of the field for the pre-game coin toss.

Presumably, as the introductions were made to the opponents, everyone would recognize Unitas and Marchetti, but when it came to Hawkins, the response—according to local legend—would be, "captain who?" As a result, Hawkins became known with great affection as "Captain Who?"

On game days, I usually got to Memorial Stadium a couple of hours before kickoff. If I were doing network television, the TV staff had to be there about 9:30 or 10 o'clock for meetings prior to the 2 P.M. game.

I'd wander around if I had time to kill, and I'd always wind up in the Colts' locker room. Fred Schubach, the equipment man, would already be there, carefully distributing towels and making sure the uniforms were ready and the shoes shined.

One of the first early-arriving players would always be Marchetti. Wearing shower shoes, shell pants, and T-shirt, he would pace from one end of the locker room to the other.

As he went back and forth, Gino never spoke to anyone as he built up the intensity he felt he needed to play the game. I never volunteered a "hello" or "how are you?" or any kind of spoken message. I just stayed out of his way and went about my business.

Linebacker Bill Pellington was another who put on his "game face." The Pellington of Sunday was not the same guy you saw Monday through Saturday. On Sunday mornings, he had the most piercing, devastating blue eyes ever seen on a human being. There was nothing but sheer rage, absolute pure anger.

Ain't the Beer Cold!

Defensive tackle Artie Donovan would not move around the locker room. He'd just sit on a stool in front of his locker. That's where my wavy-haired spotter Bob Robertson and I would find him.

Artie would usually greet us with, "Here comes the Hawk (remember my nose) and his buddy, 'Curls'—tell me a story."

So, I'd tell him one of the dumbest, crudest jokes I'd heard during the week. Artie would laugh and say, "that's pretty good," and then go into the men's room and lose everything in his stomach (and that was no joke).

That's how the nerves affected Artie before every game. He was so uptight, the only way he could get a little relief was to upchuck. Then, he was then ready for a little confrontation.

Whenever the Colts traveled to San Francisco for a game, if the bus went past anything connected to the University of San Francisco, Gino Marchetti's alma mater, the guys would yell, "That's where they retired Gino's grades!" (In case you've forgotten, Gino wound up a millionaire after hitting it big in the fast-food business).

Most of the Colts looked big enough to be pro football players, even in street clothes. But there two who didn't fit the stereotyped mold: Raymond Berry and Jimmy Orr. They could have fooled the panel on the TV game show, "What's My Line."

In fact, Berry, who looked like a college professor, did in fact stump the panel one night when it couldn't guess his occupation.

Bennett Cerf, the resident sports buff on the panel, wanted to know if John Unitas had been hurt in the championship game that day against the New York Giants. But he showed he didn't know anymore about the pronunciation of John's name than panelists Dorothy Kilgallen or Arlene Francis when he asked, "How is Mr. *'Yoon-i-tass'*?" (For the uniformed, it's *"You-nite-us."*)

Raymond had a good sense of humor. He didn't show it often, but it surfaced once when I heard that he was getting married and asked if the bride-to-be was a football fan.

"I don't know," said Raymond, keeping things in perspective, "but she can run a projector." With Raymond's propensity for

My Introduction to the NFL

reviewing game films of opponents, you can be sure his wife wore out the projector.

I was involved in a post-game incident at a Detroit bar one day after a game against the Lions. Guard Danny Sullivan had dressed quickly and since we had some time before the bus left, we talked about getting a beer. Sully said he knew of a bar that wasn't in the best of neighborhoods, but since it was close to Tiger Stadium, we took off for the joint.

As soon as we were served while standing at the bar, Sully started to complain.

"That S.O.B.," he said, "just spread me on a piece of bread, made a sandwich of me and ate me all afternoon." I asked if he were talking about Alex Karras and Sully, who was a pretty good offensive lineman, confirmed my guess and continued berating himself.

Just then a fight broke out at the other end of the bar, and one of the guys was wielding a knife. I've got news for you, and I'm very proud to report this, I got to the front door almost as soon as my pro athlete companion.

There was another fight after a Colts-Lions game in Baltimore, but for an entirely different reason. Lenny Moore had made an incredible catch over defensive back Dick "Night Train" Lane in the closed end of Memorial Stadium with time running out, putting the Colts ahead.

But Detroit had time for another play after the ensuing kickoff and Jim Gibbons caught a pass to win the game for the Lions. Many Colts fans had already left the stadium, convinced that the win was in the bag. When informed that the Colts had lost, police told me, fans had engaged in three or four nasty fights.

There were a lot of diverse personalities on the Colts, but they all came together for a superb 23-17 victory over the New York Giants in the 1958 NFL championship game on December 28, 1958.

The title game at Yankee Stadium, decided in sudden death for the first time, was hailed by *Sports Illustrated* as the "best football game ever played" (but downgraded in 1995 by the same

Ain't the Beer Cold!

publication in a list of "best ever" games). Most of the Colts thought the title game had been surpassed by their come-from-behind victory over San Francisco at Baltimore several weeks earlier, after trailing 27-7 at halftime.

The sudden death game, witnessed by some 50 million people on television, probably did more to establish the NFL as a TV property than any other game played previously or since.

Anyone who watched the telecast, particularly those from Baltimore, will remember the 20-yard field goal by Steve Myhra of the Colts with seven seconds left in regulation time which tied the score at 17-17 and sent the game into overtime.

Also unforgettable was the nearly perfect 80-yard drive drive engineered by Unitas, which ended with fullback Alan Ameche going through a huge hole on a slant off right tackle from one yard out.

With the Colts about to make history, the world seemed to come to an end in the NBC television booth for me and my broadcast partner, Chris Shenkel. We lost the picture!

The booth was filled with people but it was up to us to fill in with an audio description. It apparently wasn't a serious technical problem, but how could we stop the action? We wondered if the Colts were going to come out of the huddle and score without anyone seeing it!

All of a sudden, a spectator came running out to the middle of the field, a somewhat crazed Colts fan who wanted to be there to congratulate the winners. Referee Ron Gibbs had no choice and did the only logical thing; he called time while the spectator was escorted from the playing field.

The delay was just long enough to get the plug back in and the picture on the air so the TV audience could see Ameche ramble over the goal line.

I took advantage of this incident in later banquet talks, to offer a little fabrication. I said the guy who ran onto the field wasn't a Colts fan, but a highly paid NBC executive who knew that was the only way to get the game stopped while repairs were made. Banquet audiences loved it.

112

My Introduction to the NFL

On the play before Ameche scored, Unitas took what was criticized as an unnecessary gamble by tossing a pass to tight end Jim Mutscheller in the right flat.

Unitas, the gambler, thought it was a sure bet. Noting the Giants were playing for the run, with the linebacker head-up on Mutscheller, told the tight end to get outside quickly. "All I had to do," Unitas said, "was flip it up in the air he'd catch it." And, that's what Mutscheller did, setting up the winning TD.

Mutscheller had always been one of my favorite athletes. He wasn't nearly the size as today's tight ends, but he was quick off the line, a good solid blocker and a good pass catcher. He also provided me with good advice in evaluating players.

When we were once discussing how the Colts weren't able to execute some things on offense, Jim reminded me: "You know, those other guys out there are pretty good, too." In other words, give the other guys their due. I've tried to remember that and I'm grateful to Jim for setting it in my mind all those years ago.

The game that meant so much to Baltimore fans and the entire NFL was worth a winners' share of only $4,700 and the losers got just $3,100 each.

When the Colts arrived back in Baltimore that night at Friendship International Airport (now Baltimore-Washington International or BWI), they were met by a surging mass of humanity that was estimated to range anywhere from 15,000 to 25,000 strong.

I came back to the airport on the National Brewing Co.'s private plane with Jerry Hoffberger and his close friend, insurance agent Carle Jackson.

There was a standing rule that no alcoholic beverages were to be served on the plane, but the rule was relaxed that night in view of the championship. Then the serious celebration started once we got away from the airport.

But it wasn't an easy trip from the terminal to the Baltimore-Washington Parkway. Because of the massive crowd waiting for the team, there were cars parked on both sides along every inch of the roadway. When the bus carrying the players tried to leave, there were still fans hanging onto the roof. Women in the crowd screamed in the crush and after the crowd dispersed, lots of women's shoes were left on the lot.

Then it was on to Hasslinger's Restaurant on 25th Street, where Hoffberger hosted a victory party. It was there that Bob Robertson and Bailey Goss decided to call home and let their wives know of their whereabouts. Bob said he'd ask his wife Helen to call my wife to give her a report on me.

But Bob and Bailey, both well over 200 pounds, went downstairs and tried to use the same telephone booth at the same time, with disastrous results. Before long, a restaurant employee came to Hoffberger and reported that two of his guests had destroyed the phone booth and moved it off of its moorings. Jerry apologized profusely and promised that the phone would be put back in its original condition.

From the restaurant, we went to general manager Don Kellett's house, where our wives met us and joined in the continuing celebration and destruction.

On the way out to go home, Robby backed the car over Kellett's mail box. The next day, when we finally realized what we had done, we returned and did a repair job.

The following New Year's Eve Robby and I, accompanied by our wives, went to Kellett's home for a party. We were about to enter the house when Robby said we ought not to take any chances when it was time to leave. So we went back to the driveway, rocked the mail box back and forth, yanked it from its moorings, and carried it into his clubroom.

"Red," I told Kellett, "put this thing in the corner—we don't want to do it again."

Kellett, once the athletic director at the University of Pennsylvania and who was 0-for-9 as an infielder with the Boston Red Sox in 1934, had been hand-picked by NFL Commissioner Bert Bell to be the general manager under Colts owner Carroll Rosenbloom.

There were the usual owner-general manager disagreements, and the friendship deteriorated over the years.

I recall one year in San Francisco, where we had gone to play

My Introduction to the NFL

the 49ers, when Rosenbloom had a Thanksgiving Day party and invited the players, the media, and anyone else who was traveling with the team. But he didn't invite Kellett.

I told Robby about the oversight and we agreed to find Don and have a private dinner downtown. So, we picked up Don and started making the rounds, having a drink here and a snack there.

About an hour after we had gone, reporter John Steadman asked for us at the Rosenbloom party and no one seemed to know where we were. Then John asked for Kellett and was told he hadn't been invited. That didn't sit too well with John, either, so he took off to find us.

That turned into one of the better nights I've ever had on the road. The three original members of the wandering group wound up at an Italian restaurant and Steadman caught up with us after working his way through about seven bars in his persistent search.

The four of us had one great evening, and one of my fondest recollections was of Robby dancing with a waitress and leading her toward the kitchen until Steadman called out: "Come back, that's not on the menu."

Robby ran a couple of gas stations in the Baltimore area, and it was at one of those that he saw the last of the Colts' recalcitrant running back, Joe Don Looney.

Looney, who later died in an automobile accident, more than lived up to his surname with his actions off the field. Kellett would get calls at two or three in the morning, reporting on some of Looney's escapades.

Kellett finally had enough and decided to send Looney packing, feeling he didn't fit the mold of a Colts' player.

Looney left his apartment after breaking up the door and the furniture (another team expense) and stopped at Robby's station for gas. When he paid the bill, Joe Don asked directions for his home state of Texas. Robby pointed down York Road and said, "That way." Joe Don turned and rode off into the sunset like the hero (villain?) in a western film.

115

Chapter 11

On the Road with Crosby, Hope, and Others

Broadcasting for a team during a baseball season involves a lot more time and travel than football.

On most trips for the NFL Colts we traveled from Baltimore on Saturday to give the players time to work out in the other city that day, and returned immediately after the game on Sunday. In baseball, a roadtrip, particularly in the old days, could last two weeks or more. Players and members of the media have much more direct contact, leading to many more anecdotes to store in the memory bank.

While on the road in baseball, the traveling secretary acts as a surrogate mother, arranging departure times, bus connections at the airport, hotel accommodations, and game tickets for the players at each stop on the trip.

Phil Itzoe of the Orioles is considered the exemplary traveling secretary, a job he has served with great distinction since replacing Bob Brown at the start of the 1968 season.

When he took the job, Phil agreed with general manager Frank Cashen to start at a lower salary if he could share in post-season benefits enjoyed by the players—a wise move, considering the talent level of the club in those days.

As a result, when the Orioles finished second in 1968 to the

116

On the Road with Crosby, Hope, and Others

Detroit Tigers, Phil picked up an extra $1,900 from the club and more than $14,000 after the pennant-winning season of 1969. Phil said that "bonus" exceeded his salary for the entire year.

But that windfall set off alarm bells and Major League Baseball interceded to set a limit on how much a traveling secretary could be paid. Unofficially, at least in Baltimore, that became known as "The Itzoe Rule."

So, when the O's again won the pennant in 1970, the club was limited to paying Phil only $7,000 extra. The Orioles' players, however, showed their appreciation of Phil's tireless efforts on their behalf, and voted him another $8,000 from their winners' share of the World Series' pool.

MLB objected to the players' move but Brooks Robinson, then the O's players rep, is said to have responded, "It's our money and we'll do with it what we want." Give Brooksie credit for another great play!

Itzoe, the team's former assistant public relations director, had a gut-wrenching start in his first flight alone as traveling secretary, after making several trips with predecessor Bob Brown to learn the ropes.

Late in the 1967 season, the Orioles left Baltimore for a single make-up game in Chicago before heading on to Detroit for a three-game weekend series. It seemed to be a routine trip, so Phil was left to fly solo, so to speak.

It didn't take long for Phil to encounter his first crisis. Not long out of Baltimore, the cabin lost pressurization because the flap which was opened when the restroom was cleaned had not been refastened properly. The flap eventually worked loose and was struck by the propeller, driving it through the fuselage. Because of the loss of pressurization, the pilot was forced to make a quick descent from around 18,000 feet down to about 6,000—a sudden drop I'll never forget.

About that time, Phil took a head count of the Orioles' entourage, and came up one person short. With the loss of pressurization, the door to the restroom could not be opened from the passageway, so it was possible that someone was still inside—*maybe even had been sucked to the outside!*

Ain't the Beer Cold!

Phil and manager Hank Bauer made another head count, and came up with the same result—one short.

Tension was starting to mount when pitcher Marcellino Lopez strolled out of the cockpit, where he had been observing the crew at work! Phil was able to breathe normally once again.

The charter DC-6, a piston-engine airplane, was flown into Pittsburgh, where United replaced it with a 727 jet, which was new to the airline fleet at that time and provided the players with an unexpected treat.

Before the end of the 1967 season, however, Itzoe was to be tested again in his new capacity.

When the Orioles arrived at BWI Airport, a DC-6 they were to use was grounded by an oil problem. After an extensive wait, the intended replacement plane was found to have a fuel problem, and it was four hours before the party could take off in the second replacement.

Mindful of Phil's previous troubles, outfielder Paul Blair offered one of his famous one-liners, telling Phil: "If this how it's going to be with you as traveling secretary, I just might ask to be traded."

Itzoe was the object of an involved practical joke on the night of his 35th birthday when we were on a trip to Oakland in 1972. The late Bill O'Donnell was the instigator, and he brought along a dress belonging to his wife Pat to help set the stage.

O'Donnell's idea was to invite Phil on a blind dinner date with Jean Ryan, a red-haired friend of his wife, who was to join our party at Phil Lehr's Steak House in San Francisco. But instead of Miss Ryan the "date" was a stand-in, Ken Kimball, the producer-engineer on the Orioles' radio broadcasts.

Lou Hatter, the beat reporter for the *Baltimore Sun*, and I were in charge of outfitting Kimball, including makeup and and even a red wig to make his appearance match the advance description given by O'Donnell.

The maitre d' was so taken with our plan that he provided his office to use as a dressing room. He made periodic visits to check on our progress and even offered us drinks.

In high school football, I had good hands for *posed* action.

My intro to the major leagues, with Byrum Saam in late '40s.

With my first-born, Sandy, probably in late 1946 or early 1947.

At WITH, Baltimore, in early '50s.

Striking a "cozy pose" with Dinah Shore.

A pair of crooners…Eddie Fisher and I.

Spring training in late '50s with broadcast partners Ernie Harwell (left) and Bailey Goss (right), along with Orioles manager Paul Richards.

With fellow broadcasters Bailey Goss, Bob Wolff, and Joe Groghan, getting
ready for football.

Doing the NBC "Game of the Week" with the flamboyant former
baseball club owner Bill Veeck.

Another "Game of the Week" partner, former baseball slugger Al Rosen.

Four future Hall-of-Famers: that's me with defensive end Gino Marchetti, bowler Don Carter, and quarterback Johnny Unitas.

On the field with first baseman Boog Powell and his wife Jan.

Warren Spahn may have a good-sized "beak" but I think mine is larger.

In the booth with partner Bill O'Donnell and engineer Ken Kimball, once the "blind date" for Orioles traveling secretary Phil Itzoe.

Dad, 6-foot-1, hovered over 4-foot-10 Mom even when she wasn't sitting.

Rex Barney and I attend a 1983 Orioles function at Farragut Park in Washington, D.C.

With broadcasters Ernie Harwell and Jon Miller during the final week ceremonies at Memorial Stadium, 1991.

With Hall-of-Famer Ralph Kiner, my presenter at the Cooperstown induction. (*Photo credit: Richard Collins*)

Speaking at my Hall-of-Fame induction, 1993.

Cal and his sibling Bill share a moving moment on Cal's record-breaking night: pro to pro and brother to brother. (© *1995 Jerry Wachter Photography*)

Cal Ripken Jr., the night he set the consecutive-game record, September 6, 1995, just after the record number was posted on the warehouse beyond the right-field fence. (©*1995 Jerry Wachter Photography*)

Betty and I posing as the sheriff and the dance-hall gal while vacationing at Ocean City, Maryland.

On the Road with Crosby, Hope, and Others

When Ken was finally ready, we took him to a table where he sat with his back toward the dining room entrance to be used by O'Donnell and Itzoe when they joined us from the bar.

Despite the elaborate preparation, it didn't take long to reveal the truth—not with Kimball's face. "It was the ugliest 'woman' I ever saw," was the later summation of Itzoe, whose good eyesight belied his blind date status.

The ensuing laughter was a bit rowdy, but perhaps the sight that we treasured most was provided by a guy seated across from Kimball who twice dropped his napkin and bent over in an attempt to get a free look up Ken's dress!

On another trip, O'Donnell and I, along with Hatter, Itzoe, and Kimball went to Lowry's roast beef house in Los Angeles, and we spent about an hour in the cocktail lounge waiting to be seated for dinner.

Finally they called us and Ken bolted into the middle of the booth, with two guys on either side. The waitress dropped off the menus and after we settled down, we ordered a round of drinks.

As the waitress approached to take meal orders, Kimball announced that he had to go to the restroom. For more than an hour, we had been right next to a restroom in the lounge; *NOW, Ken gets the urge* and has to crawl out from his seat in the middle!

That was Ken—always living on the edge. I recall an incident in Milwaukee when Tom Skibosh, the Brewers' public relations director, came into the booth looking for something. Ken jumped up and hit Tom in the face with the door.

"I'll kill that S.O.B.," Tom muttered. Bill O'Donnell and I agreed: "Do us a favor and do it where we can see it."

At a gathering in a Minnesota hotel one night when the lines were flying thick and fast, Ken several times followed someone's clever remark with, "I wish I had said that!" and that is the statement that has lived down through the years long after everything else said that night had been forgotten.

In 1969 or 1970, when we went to Minneapolis for the American League Championship Series against the Twins, I was among a bunch of guys who went out one night for massages that ended with massive applications of body powder. I'll never forget the sight when we left to go back to the hotel, when giant puffs of powder arose after each step. I think the biggest puffs came from Gordon Beard's size 13 shoes.

On occasion, we'd call friends back in the Maryland area in the middle of the night and ask ridiculous questions. Like asking Cliff "Homer" Van Roby, when it was 3 A.M. or so in his hometown of Cumberland, Maryland, "What are you doing, 'Homer,' watching a little TV?"

One such episode backfired when we called Gordon Beard at about midnight on the West Coast (3 A.M. where Gordon was sleeping in Annapolis, Maryland.). Manager Earl Weaver asked Gordon how the Detroit Tigers (who were then fighting the O's for first place) had done in the second game of their doubleheader the previous evening. Then Earl turned the phone over to me and I asked the score of a high school game (probably as an irritant).

I learned later that Gordon had called the Associated Press for the results we had requested and then set his alarm clock for 6 A.M. So it was 3 A.M. on the West Coast when he returned our call with the results, asking the hotel operator to stay on the line while she rang each room (apparently Gordo's motto was: Don't get mad; get even).

I didn't always travel with the team. Sometimes I went alone when the club left Baltimore at a time inconvenient for me and I could still get there in time for the next game by departing later, or when I had an appointment on an off-day on the road and didn't depart until later.

On one such occasion (I think we were in Minneapolis), the Orioles were scheduled to fly to California following a damaging loss that would have felt even worse being rehashed during a long flight on a prop plane.

I told traveling secretary Phil Itzoe that if he didn't mind, I was going to fly down to Chicago and pick up a later jet plane. Phil said that sounded like a good idea and wished that he could have done the same.

When I checked in at Chicago and took my seat, all the stewardesses were excited and scurrying around saying things like, "Do you know who you're sitting with?" or "You're going to have a wonderful trip—Bing Crosby is your seatmate."

Well, it turned out to be a memorable trip all right—much better than I could have expected.

Bing had been in North Dakota, or someplace, for a remake of the movie *Stagecoach*. He had a growth of whiskers and looked kind of grungy, and the little luggage he had was stored in the overhead rack. He was the last person to board.

We both started reading the sports pages and eventually we engaged in conversation. As we talked, I told him what my job was—I was already familiar with his occupation.

We both ordered a drink and then another, and then—well, what else are you going to do from Chicago to Los Angeles? Never had a thing to eat. Everytime the stewardess asked if we wanted anything to eat, Bing would shake the ice cubes in his raised glass and she'd come with more drinks. Along the way, Bing invited me to go fishing with him in Mexico some day.

After an hour or so into the flight, I said with all the great movies he had made and with all the wonderful songs he had sung, why would just one episode from an average movie stay with me all these days?

When Bing asked what movie I had in mind, I said, "I can't tell you the name of it, but I can set the scene for you."

"Please do."

"You were sitting on the ground alongside a convertible automobile—I guess you'd call it a roadster in those days, repairing an innertube. Sitting of the back of the car was one of the most beautiful blondes (Frances Farmer) I had ever seen in my life and you sang a great song—at least, I thought it was a great song."

"You can't be that old," Bing said, referring to what I learned later was the 1936 movie, *Rhythm on the Range*, in which the late Martha Raye made her feature film debut.

Bing then asked if I remembered the name of the song and I said, "You're damned right I do—it was ' I Can't Escape From You.' And, just like that, Bing Crosby *sang it for me* right there on that westbound plane! I assure you, he had an appreciative audience.

Several years later (1971), the Orioles were in the World Series against the Pittsburgh Pirates, and Bill O'Donnell and I were in the booth prior to one of the games. Into the booth came Bing, who then owned a piece of the Pirates, accompanied by a public relations person from the club. When he was introduced to Bill, Bing gave him a big smile, said how happy he was to meet him and expressed the hope that we'd have a good game to broadcast.

Then the P.R. guy turns to me and says, "Bing, this is Bill's partner, Chuck Thompson."

"How do you do, Bing," I said. "Glad to see you again."

He looked at me kind of quizzically at first and then said, "Don't I know you?"

"Yes," I said, "we shared a helluva plane ride to Los Angeles."

"I can't escape from you—and that's about right," Bing said. Then he laughed and said, "Glad to see you again."

As a postscript, I must add that I never got the chance to go fishing with him in Mexico.

Along the way in my career, I also met the other two stars of the "Road" series of movies—Bob Hope and Dorothy Lamour.

I met Hope when I was doing a football game for CBS-TV. They wanted him to do a halftime interview and as we climbed down into the mezzanine overhang at Baltimore's Memorial Stadium, Bob said, "Do you think they'd mind if I plug my show?"

"Mr. Hope," I said, "if you're good enough to come on at halftime for this network, how in the world are they going to stop you?"

"Are you sure it's not going to get you into any trouble?"

No problem. I led him into the promo during the interview, and all went well.

The meeting with Dorothy Lamour was a bit more casual. I was having dinner in Baltimore one night at "Danny's" when owner Danny Dickman came to the table and said Miss Lamour was there with her mother and they wanted to meet me. It turned out that Dorothy, who lived in the Baltimore area at that time, was a pretty good Orioles fan and had heard me broadcasting the games.

Crosby, Hope, and Lamour—you never know who you'll run into broadcasting sports. But there were also the games to report, and sometimes the action on the field was just as entertaining as the encounters with the celebrities—even though you don't know all of the story at first.

Boog Powell once lined into a triple play when he smashed a pitch back through the middle that Detroit pitcher Denny McLain snared simply because his glove happened to be in the right spot after he released the ball. Denny caught the ball and wheeled to double Paul Blair off second base, and the relay to first retired Frank Robinson for a triple play.

In another game, Boog's smash off another McLain delivery didn't threaten the pitcher. Instead, the ball struck the transmitter tower atop the Tiger Stadium roof. Denny was enthralled; he watched the flight of the ball, then shook his head as Boog rounded the bases.

The next time Boog came to bat, as he planted his rear foot in the box and prepared to move in with his right foot, McLain rolled the ball toward the plate and shouted: "Hey, hit that, you big fat S.O.B." I saw McLain rolling the ball when he did it, but Boog had to fill me in later with Denny's comment.

In another Orioles-Tigers game in Detroit, Frank again was on first and Blair on second when an Orioles' batter hit a ball into the right-center field gap. Frank knew the ball was going to drop safely because of his better angle, and was off and running.

Paul held up momentarily around the shortstop position until he was certain the ball wouldn't be caught.

By that time, Frank was only about two steps behind Paul. They rounded third, bang-bang, and I was amazed the speedy Blair wasn't opening up any daylight on Robinson. As they arrived at the plate, one slid to the right side and the other to the left—and both were safe!

I'd never seen that kind of play before and I couldn't wait to get to the clubhouse to ask some questions. I asked three or four guys and they all said they'd seen it before, but most of the time, both runners were tagged out. For Frank, however, it was a first-time experience.

There must have been something about the Tigers that brought out the bizarre in the Orioles. Here's another Tiger Stadium memory:

There's maybe only one thing that will make me lose my concentration when I'm describing a ballgame, and that's when a batter loses control of the bat and it goes tumbling end over end into the seats. That's almost as scary as a beaning. As I'm describing such an incident, I'm thinking, "God, I hope nobody's hurt."

In this particular game, with Paul Blair on third base, the bat slips out of Frank Robinson's hands and heads for the seats behind the Tigers' dugout. I was slightly terrified but I kept talking, and Frank was standing in the batter's box holding his breath that no one would be hurt.

Blair was also tranfixed as he stared into the stands. But there was one player still alert—catcher Bill Freehan, who caught the ball that Robinson had missed on his swing.

Freehan calmly jogged down the third-base line, where Blair stood two or three steps off the bag, and said, "Hey, Paulie, look what I've got" and made the tag.

Paul went a little berzerk and said he couldn't be called out because—and he had a legitimate beef—"if I'm out, I'll have to go in that dugout and (manager Earl) Weaver's going to kill me."

Blair, nicknamed "Motormouth" for his incessant chatter, was an engaging personality with a great sense of humor. Once, coming out of the hot sun into the dugout, he looked at his arms and said, "I used to be a teasing bronze—now I'm turning into dark chocolate."

On the team bus in New York, Orioles outfielders Frank Robinson and Sam Bowens were looking at a newspaper which included a picture of Frank taken during the previous day's game.

"Hey, Blair," Frank called out, "Sam says I look like George Scott (Boston's rookie first baseman) in this picture. You know I don't look like Scott."

On the Road with Crosby, Hope, and Others

"That's all right, Sam," called out Brooks Robinson in defense of Bowen's judgment. "I think he looks like Scott, too."

Another opening for Blair. "That's different," he said in response to Brooksie. "You think we all look alike."

Scott, one of my favorite guys, had a unique way of expressing himself, and not all his terminology could be recounted in print.

In the Milwaukee park in 1974 there was a gate which led to the bullpen area in right-center field. Scott, then playing for the Brewers, hit a shot to that area one day, Blair broke at the crack of the bat, made a spectacular leaping catch as he hit the door and knocked it open, and held onto the ball.

It was the final out in the O's 11-inning victory during a torrid stretch run in September that led to their fifth Eastern Division championship in the first six years of divisional play.

The next evening, Scott walked over to the Orioles' dugout during batting practice, paced up and down a little, then started to shake his head.

"You understand me," he said, to no one in particular, "no other (deleted) living human being could have caught that (deleted) ball." Having spoken his piece without mentioning Blair's name, George walked over to the Milwaukee dugout and sat down.

Former Orioles coach Jim Frey relayed another now-it-can-be-told story that occurred in 1980, when he was managing Kansas City and the pitcher for Cleveland was Ross Grimsley, who had pitched for the Orioles while Frey was in Baltimore.

"My batters were taking a lot of pitches, flinching and swinging and missing. I knew Ross was good, but not that good—then I got to thinking about his success with KY Jelly when he was with the Orioles.

"After he retired the first nine batters or so, I went out to the plate and said to the umpire, 'This guy's cheating, there's no way in the world this guy can make my hitters look this bad. We have the best hitting club (the Royals led the league with a .286 mark that year) and against this guy, we can't even make contact. I know he's cheating.'"

Ain't the Beer Cold!

Frey, when he recalled the story years later was agitated again, and continued: "When the umpire, I think it was Bill Kunkel or Larry Barnett, asked what I thought Ross was doing, I had a ready answer. 'All I know is that in Baltimore he used that (deleted) grease. George Bamberger (the O's pitching coach) taught him and I used to warm him up in the bullpen.'

"When the umpire started out to the mound, Ross ran into the dugout and up the runway. Three or four minutes later he came back and said he was ready to go. I don't think he got another out."

Grimsley was 4-5 with Cleveland in 1980 after being acquired on July 11th, and was 1-2 in his final big-league season with the Orioles in 1982. So, in fact, he did little of anything after Frey's complaint.

A couple of years later, Frey was in a supermarket in the Baltimore area during the winter with his wife when someone came up from behind and grabbed him around the neck. "I could hardly talk," said Frey, "but I did manage to gasp, 'who is it?'

"I turned and it was Ross Grimsley. He said, 'S.O.B, you ran me right out of the game.' But he wasn't really angry."

Before his retirement, the lefthander won 124 games and was in double figures in wins eight times, including 18 for Baltimore in 1974 and 20 for Montreal in 1978 (he remains the only 20-game winner in Expos history).

The Orioles have provided many reels of highlights during my years of broadcasting, but if I had to choose the most memorable on-field performance, my choice would be their four-game sweep over the Los Angeles Dodgers in the 1966 World Series.

That was something akin to the Colts winning their first NFL championship, as far as the excitement generated in the city was concerned.

The Dodgers had swept the New York Yankees in the 1963 fall classic, came back in 1965 to edge the Minnesota Twins in a seven-game series, and had Hall-of-Fame pitchers Sandy Koufax and Don Drysdale ready to throw at the Orioles in Baltimore's first post-season appearance. There was talk of a sweep when the series opened, but the experts (and Los Angeles fans) expected it would be by the Dodgers.

But in the top of the first inning of the first game, in Los Angeles, Drysdale walked Russ Snyder with one out, then Frank and Brooks Robinson hit consecutive home runs for a 3-0 lead and the Orioles never trailed throughout the Series. The Robinsons had combined to hit 72 homers during the season, but never back-to-back since the second game of 1966.

Moe Drabowsky relieved Dave McNally in the third inning after the Orioles' starter walked three batters in a row. Moe walked his first batter to force in a run, but over the final six and two-thirds innings he allowed but one hit and struck out 11, including six straight in the fifth and sixth innings as the O's won, 5-2. Both the 11 and the six in a row are still World Series records for a reliever.

In the second game, the Dodgers made six errors, three by center fielder Willie Davis in the fifth inning, a handicap that even the incomparable Koufax couldn't overcome. The Orioles won 6-0 on a four-hitter by Jim Palmer, who became the youngest hurler to throw a World Series shutout. In fact, it was Jim's first shutout in the major leagues and only his sixth complete game of 1966.

Back to Baltimore we came, where a fan greeting the team at BWI Airport held up a sign which read, "Lose just one. I've got tickets for Monday."

But the Orioles didn't comply, ending the Series with consecutive 1-0 shutouts on Saturday and Sunday. Wally Bunker, age 22, allowed six hits in the third game, making only 91 pitches in his first shutout and third complete game of 1966. The Orioles only had three hits, but one was a homer by Paul Blair, at 22 the youngest position player in the Series.

Dave McNally, who allowed the only Los Angeles' runs in the sweep, came back to throw the third straight shutout in the final game. Three of the Dodgers four hits were followed by double plays and one of Baltimore's four hits was a homer by Frank Robinson, again off Drysdale.

The Dodgers set World Series record lows with two runs,

17 hits, and a team batting average of .147. The 33 consecutive scoreless innings also broke a mark of 28 set by the New York Giants in 1905, the last time there were three straight shutouts.

One last memory of that Series. On the team bus back to the hotel after the first game, the Orioles were talking about all the celebrities they had spotted in the L.A. crowd. When someone mentioned Frank Sinatra, second baseman Davey Johnson said he hadn't seen Frank who was behind the team's dugout.

"If you no see Sinatra," said shortstop Luis Aparicio, "how you gonna see Koufax curveball?"

Well, in Game 2, Johnson had the last hit off Koufax before he was relieved in the seventh inning—and the last he yielded in his Hall-of-Fame career. When Davey was named the Orioles' manager in 1995, he told a news conference that it was his World Series hit that convinced Koufax that it was time to retire.

The Orioles also played in the World Series in 1969, 1970, 1971, 1979, and 1983, but like the first kiss, I'll always be fondest of the first one.

Chapter 12

Characters and High Jinks

I met a host of characters during my career as a broadcaster and I've seen a lot of high jinks, many of which I was involved in personally.

Among my favorite characters would be Bill Veeck, John Lowenstein, Mike Flanagan, Moe Drabowsky, Norm Van Brocklin, and Ellis Clary, with lesser roles played by the likes of Jim Gentile, Warren Spahn, and Luke Appling, and personal friends Bailey Goss and Bob Robertson.

Veeck, the irrepressible owner of the St. Louis Browns, Cleveland Indians, and Chicago White Sox, lit up any gathering with his wit and sparkling conversation on a wide range of subjects. He was obviously a well-read man and intelligent—the kind of owner we'd like to have more of in baseball today.

Veeck, of course, is known for signing midget Eddie Gaedel to a contract for the Browns in 1951. Little Eddie did as Bill had intended, walking in his lone plate appearance as the leadoff batter before being replaced by a pinch runner.

The flamboyant Veeck, elected to the Baseball Hall of Fame for meritorious service as an executive, also introduced the exploding scoreboard and any number of special promotions that have become a permanent part of the baseball scene.

In short, the late Veeck thought that time spent at the ballpark should be fun—to entertain the fans so that they would want to come back. What a novel approach!

But Bill also had a very serious side and he was very sensitive about one particular issue—that children should not be allowed in barrooms. The only other person I know who felt as strongly was Cal Ripken, Sr., and the irony was that both were inveterate beer drinkers.

I recall a night in a Detroit bar, when a young father came in with his son and asked Cal to sign an autograph for the boy, who was somewhere between six and eight years old. Cal refused and the man left with his son. After a few seconds, Cal walked out and explained his decision, that the bar was not a proper place for the boy, and then honored the autograph request.

Veeck delivered the same message one afternoon at a Milwaukee bar but, as might be expected, he used a more spectacular approach. We were in the bar prior to going out to watch a game that night, where we would pick up some background material for our NBC "Game of the Week" network broadcast the next day (sometimes I worked with Bill, other times with Al Rosen).

A fellow, with his son of about eight in tow, was expounding about his exploits and his alleged feats seemed to become more outrageous with each sip of beer. He told of his prowess at bowling, baseball—whatever.

It was obvious that Veeck was disturbed, both by the father's bragging and the fact that the boy was in the bar. Finally, he asked me to get an ice pick from the bartender. I couldn't figure out why he wanted an ice pick, but I went up and borrowed one.

As the father continued his monologue, Bill raised his voice and said, "Hey, young man, come here a minute will you, please." The father gave his nodding approval.

When the lad approached, Veeck took the ice pick and jammed it into his wooden leg, which replaced a limb he lost as a Marine during a World War II invasion in the Pacific.

"Ask your father if he can do that!" Bill said. Bill had made his point, so to speak, as the braggart and son left quickly.

But it was abundantly clear that Veeck had his own ideas

Characters and High Jinks

about beer drinking on his own, and it didn't have to be in a bar. The first time I met Bill was in his hotel room in Miami, where he was having breakfast while soaking the stump of his leg in the bathtub. For breakfast, he had a glass of orange juice, four tiny sausage links—and a six-pack of beer!

John Lowenstein was a real piece of work; in fact, he retained his delightful rascality in his role as an analyst for Orioles games on the Home Team Sports cable broadcasts, during an 11-year stint that ended after the 1995 season.

Orioles manager Earl Weaver, who never made it to the major leagues as a player, was trying to explain to catcher Dan Graham one day how to approach hitting. The advice went something like this: "If you look for a certain pitch, then sit on it and wait—you can handle it, even if it's a curveball." Then Earl looked toward Lowenstein and added, "Right, John?"

That wasn't exactly the approach of "Brother Lo," who responded: "In 12 years up here, I never looked for anything but that (deleted) fastball."

One night in Texas, after John hit a game-winning homer, he was approached by a young reporter who obviously didn't understand John's sometimes flaky nature and asked him to tell about the home run. The conversation went something like this:

"Were you in the ballpark? Didn't you see what happened?"

"Well, yeh."

"Did you see the home run?"

"Yeh."

"Did you see the ball go over the fence?"

"Yeh."

"Then what the hell do you want me to tell you about it?"

Somewhat taken aback, the young man tried to change the subject and said, "John, tell me something."

"Now what?"

"Who do you think started the fad of catching the ball one-handed?"

Without hesitation, John deadpanned, "I think it was a guy named Pete Gray."

Others in the group laughed, but apparently the reporter wasn't old enough to be familiar with Gray, the one-armed outfielder for the St. Louis Browns in 1945.

On another occasion, Lowenstein gave this description of a homer sailing over the fence: "It tends to immobilize the outfielder."

Once, when John was struck in the head by a thrown ball, he said the incident would probably satisfy his dad's lifelong desire that he have his head examined.

In a 1980 game, John was struck in the back of the neck by a relay throw after doubling home the tying run in the seventh inning against Oakland. John was knocked out for a time as the ball caromed into center field, allowing Al Bumbry to score the go-ahead run.

The Memorial Stadium crowd was silenced, expecting the worst, before John revived and again seized the moment. With the applause building as he was carried off the field on a stretcher, John suddenly bolted to an upright position and raised his arms with clenched fists above his head just before disappearing into the dugout. The crowd may have been "taken," but showed its appreciation by cheering loud and long.

"It was something I had wanted to do ever since I saw Norm Cash do it in 1970," John said. "I vowed to do it if I ever had a shot."

Ray Miller, the former Orioles' pitching coach now in that capacity for the Pittsburgh Pirates, perhaps summed up Lowenstein's off-the-wall antics perfectly when he said, "We should all be grateful that John allows us to be a part of his world."

Pitcher Mike Flanagan was king of the topical one-liners, the kind of guy who eased the tension in the clubhouse and in the dugout. He was lightning quick with a line that fit the occasion.

When 5-9 manager Earl Weaver didn't get a joke, Mike called it a "six-foot joke" because it was over his head. On an Orioles' charter flight in 1983, the year after Weaver had retired for the first time, the usual shrimp hors d'oeuvres were not aboard. That prompted second baseman Rich Dauer to ask, "Where's the shrimp?" and Flanagan was ready with an appropo response: "He's in Miami, playing golf."

Characters and High Jinks

Mike also specialized in nicknames. Jerry Hairston of the White Sox who had a receding hairline was dubbed "Nohairston." John Castino of the Twins was called "Clams." And, when Tony Solaita was released by the Blue Jays, he became Tony "Obsoleto."

One day, the Orioles' mascot, called "The Bird," fell off the dugout roof, and Mike quickly sized up the situation: "Take two worms and call me in the morning."

Outfielder Dan Ford, not known for his defensive prowess, turned his glove over to trainer Ralph Salvon for repairs and Mike suggested that Ralph get a welder to handle the job.

Moe Drabowsky, another pitcher, was more into practical jokes. In a 1966 series at Kansas City, where Moe had pitched before joining the Orioles, he phoned the A's bullpen and told coach Bobby Hofman to "get Krausse hot." Thinking the call came from manager Alvin Dark, Hofman told Lew Krausse to get ready.

Later, Moe called and said, "OK, sit him down." The guys in the Baltimore bullpen were laughing but the A's didn't realize what was happening until Moe called again, asked for Krausse, and said, "Are you warm, Lew?" Krausse recognized Moe's voice.

Drabowsky was busy in relief the next night but on Sunday he again had some time on his hands, so he called the bullpen and imitated owner Charlie Finley. "I just got back in town," Moe said, "and I read about the calls you got Friday night. I'd like to hear your version of the episode."

Hofman launched into a detailed account before he became suspicious and identified mischievous Moe.

Moe was a stockbroker on the side and one of his best customers was Finley, who died early in 1996. Finley was wise to the stockbroker language but Moe's sales pitches were sometimes confusing to his former Orioles teammate, Frank Robinson.

Frank didn't want to risk much on speculation, but after listening to Moe, he said, "Okay, fine—I'll take 2,000."

Later at his home in California, Frank recieved a bill form Moe and practically fell off his chair. Frank thought he was

Ain't the Beer Cold!

investing $2,000; Moe thought he was buying 2,000 shares, and there was an appreciable difference that had to be adjusted.

I thought Moe's greatest prank occurred on an Orioles' roadtrip, to Seattle. We arrived late at night to find that the hotel was being renovated and repainted. All the numbers had been removed from the doors and replaced temporarily by numbers drawn in chalk.

Moe went one extra, diabolical step. He erased the temporary numbers on every room but his own and wrote in different numbers. Many of the Orioles were stymied because their keys wouldn't work in the locks. There was an instant pandemonium and it took a massive effort to straighten out the mess. But everyone knew who caused it.

Norm Van Brocklin was one of the premier quarterbacks in the National Football League who later went on to coaching. The "Dutchman" was a very volatile man who was not above raising a little heck now and then. But I considered him one of the good guys in sports.

I used to host a Monday night television show in Baltimore called, "Corraling the Colts," during which films of the previous day's game where shown and analyzed by a panel of sportswriters, sportscasters, and players. The players were very cooperative and contributed much to what proved to be a successful format.

After the games on Sunday, I used to interview the visiting coach and maybe one or two of his players to be replayed on tape during the show.

On this particular Sunday, the Colts had beaten Van Brocklin's Minnesota Vikings and I was waiting outside the visitors' locker room when the door opened and there stood the seething losing coach.

As he lit a cigarette, Norm looked up and saw a familiar face—mine. He reached across the hallway, slammed me up against the wall, and snarled, "Wait till we get you S.O.B.'s out there (Minnesota)."

Well, when we went on the road to play the Vikings, quarterback John Unitas was injured and not available. It looked like a good chance that the "Dutchman" would get his revenge. But Gary Cuozzo replaced Unitas and led the Colts to victory with a club record six touchdown passes. The enraged Van Brocklin quit that night, but Minnesota officials were able to talk him back into returning the next day.

I've heard a story attributed to Van Brocklin and I'm not sure it's absolute fact, but here's what I was told:

Norm's daughter came home from college for the Christmas holidays, anxious that the family meet her fiance.

Swept up in the moment, the smiling dad hugged his daughter and held her in the air, then put her down so she could greet Mom. In the doorway stood a young man whose appearance turned off Van Brocklin because he had hair that hung down to the middle of his back.

"Young man, go get a haircut," said Norm, and shut the door. A half hour later the suitor returned, as mother and daughter were still ranting about his abrupt dismissal. The kid had gotten a haircut.

A beaming Van Brocklin placed his hands under the visitor's armpits and carried him across the threshold as he said: "Young man, you're going to be all right."

I wish I could have confirmed the story, but knowing Van Brocklin as well as I did, I could believe it even without confirmation.

You may recall that I mentioned earlier that in one of the first International League games I had broadcast, Orioles infielder Ellis Clary went after a fan in the stands.

Ellis often showed evidence of being a little unstable. One night he called Orioles owner and general manager Jack Dunn, and said he was out on the town to drown his sorrows, after coming to the conclusion that he would never return to the major leagues (he had played 223 games for Washington and the St. Louis Browns in 1942-45 and had one at-bat in the 1944 World Series). That being the case, he was going to take his own life.

Jack tried to talk him out of the idea, but Ellis insisted he had made up his mind. After much prodding, Jack made Ellis promise to sleep on it and call him back in the morning. Jack thought that would be the end of it, but when Ellis called back the next day he said he hadn't changed his mind.

"You know you're not going to do anything like that," said Jack.

"The hell I'm not. You ain't never going to hear from me again."

"If you really feel that way, I can't tell you how sorry I am. But I might as well tell you that if you really feel that way, you go right ahead. I've just traded you to Buffalo."

Well, Clary didn't commit suicide and if you ever travel through the South and get near Valdosta, Georgia, look up Clary's poolroom and you'll meet one of the most engaging, entertaining good guys who was ever involved in baseball.

Ellis never did return to the majors as a player, but he coached for the Senators in the late '50s and scouted several years for the Minnesota Twins. A few years after we first met, we crossed paths again when I was broadcasting for the Senators (1957-60) and again later when I was broadcasting a Colts' game at Memorial Stadium in Baltimore.

On that day, an usher in the broadcast booth said I had a long distance phone call from Valdosta, Georgia. It had to be Ellis, who every now and then was known to make a bet on a sporting event.

It had rained all night in Baltimore and the field was still covered prior to the Colts-Green Bay Packers NFL game. I relayed that information to Ellis and added that if the rain didn't let up, the conditions might get pretty bad in the second half.

"You mean that?"

"I'm just telling you what's going on."

"I just took the Colts and gave 14 points."

"Ellis, this is the NFL and you're talking about the Packers—I wouldn't give 14 points if the Colts were playing the Little Sisters of the Poor."

"You mean that?"

"You're darn right."

I never did find out if Ellis had gotten out of the bet, but I must tell you that the Colts won that game by a score of 56-0! So much for expert advice.

The next spring I went to Orlando, Florida, to cover the Senators training camp and the first day I put foot on the field, Ellis started.

"Here comes that old goat," he yelled, "that baseball-football expert. Anything you want to know about pro football, just ask that man—he knows it all." After that, everytime I'd see Ellis, he would simply say, "Green Bay." Somehow, I felt that even if he had gotten out of the bet, based on my counsel, he harbored no hard feelings.

Playing sports is a serious business for those involved, but it doesn't surprise me at all that those who work so hard to defeat an opponent sometimes need a pretty good sense of humor—to relieve the tension, if nothing else.

I went to Pittsburgh one weekend to do a Steelers' game for CBS-TV. As usual, I picked up a copy of the Saturday paper to bring myself up to speed for the next day's game.

In the paper was a story by Al Abrams in which he quoted defensive tackle Ernie Stautner of the Steelers (who later was enshrined into the Pro Football Hall of Fame) sounding off about the Pittsburgh fans. Stautner said the fans shouldn't get on the team even when it wasn't playing well, because times would get better. What owner Art Rooney ought to do, Ernie concluded, was move the franchise away from the fickle fans. A reaction to the story came the next day.

The CBS booth at Forbes Field was located right alongside the runway where the Steelers came out onto the field. Like most teams they had a single guy who would lead them out, and in this case it was Stautner.

When CBS gave the signal, Ernie took off and the minute he was in sight, the stands rocked. I never heard a player booed like that in my life, not even Reggie Jackson when he played for the New York Yankees against the Orioles in Baltimore.

Stautner chugged along with his head bowed until he was almost halfway across the field, when he turned to say something to one of his teammates right behind. It was then he realized that he had been left to go out on the field alone to face the hecklers!

Ain't the Beer Cold!

Jim Gentile, the slugging first baseman of the Orioles from 1961 through 1963, had a sense of humor but most of the time he was a worrywart. When things were going well for him at the plate, "Diamond Jim" would be worrying about when he might go into a slump.

Jim was hitting so well over one stretch that he was inserted into the starting lineup against the New York Yankees Hall-of-Fame lefthander Whitey Ford, who was especially difficult for a left-handed batter like Gentile.

It was a good idea in theory, perhaps, but not in practice. Jim struck out swinging three times against Whitey, the last time for the third out of the inning. As we rolled a commercial between innings, I saw Brooks Robinson come out of the dugout and toss Jim his first basemen's mitt.

Jim was visibly upset, pounding the bat against his leg as he walked. Seeing the huge mitt coming his way, Jim swung—and missed again! When we came back on the air, it was all I could do to control myself.

In a game at Kansas City, Jim made a spectacular diving stop of a hard-hit grounder along the first-base line, bringing applause even from the Kansas City fans. But Jim was so tangled up, he couldn't get to his feet and make the throw to the pitcher covering. So, he merely grabbed a handful of infield dirt and covered the ball where it lay, as sort of a lasting monument to his great stop.

Hall-of-Fame shortstop Luke Appling was a great storyteller and I was exposed to several of his yarns while he served as an Orioles' coach in 1963.

Luke was well known for his ability to foul off pitches until he got one he could handle, and he put that talent to use after the White Sox turned down his request for a dozen baseballs to give away to fans.

At batting practice the following day at Comiskey Park, Luke fouled pitch after pitch into the stands, where they were grabbed by appreciative fans and management got the message. On his second trip to the batting cage, the bat boy presented him with a box of a dozen baseballs—and Luke suddenly regained control of his swing.

Characters and High Jinks

Luke used to complain about the condition of the Comiskey Park infield, contending that the grounds crew never worked it while the team was on the road in the days of 18- to 21-day trips.

To prove his point, on the final day of a homestand, Luke took some grass seed out to his position for three or four innings and dropped them after scraping the dirt with his spikes.

On the trip home, Luke said grass would be growing at his shortstop position and a lot of money was wagered on his statement. The team returned in the early morning hours, went to the park and got a security guard to let them in. With flashlights in hand, Luke said, they went out to the field and found grass exactly as he predicted, about two inches high.

Another Hall-of-Famer I meet every so often in my travels is Warren Spahn, the Milwaukee Braves ace who, in my mind, had two claims to fame: 363 wins, the most ever for a left-handed pitcher, and a nose about the size of mine.

When I saw Warren one day in Cooperstown, I told him I had lost one of my favorite pictures, the one we had taken in Miami when we posed nose-to-nose. He said he recalled the picture and suggested we take another the next day. The cameraman was ready but it rained the next day and we didn't make connections. I have since located the photo and I've included it in this book.

Anyway, while we were talking in Cooperstown, a crowd gathered and Warren explained that we were talking about noses.

"But we don't want you to feel sorry for us; we feel sorry for you," Warren told the crowd. "What starts the minute you get up every morning? You inhale and you have to do that all day long. Chuck and I just take one sniff, and that holds us the rest of the day."

The laughs weren't confined to the athletes, by any means. Many friends and acquaintances have left lasting impressions with their free-spirited antics. Bailey Goss, who did the commercials when I was broadcasting Orioles games, was a close friend on and off the job, and was a delightful drinking and golfing companion.

We were standing outside Memorial Stadium early one morning, waiting to be picked up for a fishing trip to Maryland's

Ain't the Beer Cold!

Eastern Shore. Time was dragging and, having nothing better to do, Bailey pointed to the front of the stadium and said, "Do you think you could hit a wedge over that?" I didn't know, having never tried such an outrageous shot.

Bailey said, "let's try" and we did, after moving into the flower beds next to the metal railing alongside 33rd Street and tried to clear the 116-foot facade. Pretty soon it was raining golf balls and Bailey may have come close to achieving the goal as he was a lot better golfer and much stronger than I.

Pretty soon, a police car with its lights flashing pulls up to the curb and an officer said, "What the hell do you think you're doing?"

"We're going fishing," Bailey replied, before realizing such a remark might be misconstrued as a wise guy's crack. "Wait a minute, I didn't mean that the way it sounded—I apologize. But we are going to go fishing."

"Then why don't you go?"

"We're being picked up."

"Who in the world is going to pick you two up?"

"The governor."

That did it. The officers looked at one another in exasperation, shrugged, slammed the door and drove off.

Five minutes later, a chauffeur-driven Cadillac pulled up and we got into the car with Gov. Theodore R. McKeldin. That was the only time I ever went across the Chesapeake Bay Bridge without paying a toll.

I was involved in another impromptu golf driving exhibition one night when someone challenged me that I couldn't hit a ball over the Washington Monument near downtown Baltimore at Charles Street and Mount Vernon Square.

In my frame of mind, having just finished a few drinks at an after-hours club to the rear of the Park Plaza Hotel, nicknamed "Witches and Bitches" in honor of the bartenders and waitresses who patronized the spot, I accepted the challenge.

I opened the trunk of my car and took out a 9-iron and several balls, walked over to a grassy area across from the Park Plaza, and started pumping away from near Madison Street.

Characters and High Jinks

Quite a few balls were bouncing down Charles Street and though I couldn't see in the dark, I maintained that they all cleared the monument (I found out later the monument was 188 feet high, not counting the hill on which it stands, so my assumption may have been false).

Just as in the Memorial Stadium escapade, a police car with flashing lights pulled up and an officer jumped out. "I should have known it was you," he said. "Get the hell out of here."

In those days, a group of us would meet after a night baseball game, maybe a couple times a week, at Eddie Leonard's Spa on Charles Street, not far from the monument, for a nightcap and bull session.

On most nights, the group would include Gil Kriegel of WITH Radio, sports editor Jesse Linthicum of the *Baltimore Sun*, owner Eddie, and Irv Klein, a theatrical agent. They were fun guys to talk with and one of Eddie's hard and fast rules was that you could bet on anything, as long as you didn't exceed a nickel.

One night, someone bet that it took 50 cobblestones to reach across the street. Everyone put a nickel in the pot and then we'd be out there after midnight counting the cobblestones. The winner would be whoever came the closest to the actual number. If we argued over a sports question, Jesse Linthicum would call his staff at the Sunpapers to get the correct answer.

After I grew accustomed to Baltimore, I brought the family down from Pennsylvania and moved to the Lochearn area west of the city. We rented a house for two years, with an option to buy, but it never worked out that way and we finally moved to the house I still live in today on Timonium Road in Timonium.

I was disappointed that we couldn't stay in Lochearn because we had some good neighbors. There was a tavern on the corner of Liberty Road and Gwynn Oak Avenue where I used to meet my neighbors Bob Sharman, a salesman for the McCormick spice company and Doc Hebb, owner of the Aristocrat Dairy. We lived in three adjacent houses and late at night the neighbors could hear three garage doors slamming in succession.

Those were learning days for me covering the International

Ain't the Beer Cold!

League Orioles and U.S. Naval Academy football. I was told by officials at the academy that the worst thing I could do would be to refer to the Navy players as Middies, contending that word referred to blouses worn by young ladies. The politically correct name in those days was Midshipmen, although Middies seems sometimes to be acceptable in the '90s.

One day Bailey Goss and I had to work a luncheon downtown at the Lord Baltimore Hotel. On the way out, he suggested we have a drink. We had a lot more than one and when I next looked at my watch it was 4:30 P.M., and time to head for home.

I drove Bailey to his house and as we went up the driveway, there was his lovely wife Anne, looking more than a little upset. But Bailey jumped out and flashed his million-dollar smile while giving Anne some sweet talk.

When I started to laugh, Anne pointed a finger at me and said, "You'd better get your butt home. Rose has been calling all afternoon."

Instead, I headed back downtown, stopping first at Eddie Leonard's Spa and then made the rounds of the Blue Mirror, the Coronet, and back to the Spa. Then I was off to Love's Restaurant at 25th Street before at last going home (It seems I was frequently AWOL from home, even when not on the road!).

I was driving a used Cadillac, the model with "boobs" sticking out about a foot beyond the front bumper and an oversized tailfin behind. It was a huge car that simply would not fit into our garage. I had tried it several times.

But this night, I thought it had to fit—I would make it fit, by golly. On the other side of the back wall of the garage my wife Rose was relaxing on the sofa, watching TV, with bookcases on either side of the sofa.

I didn't get the car stopped in time and buried it into the garage wall, tossing Rose onto the floor. I got out of the car and slammed the garage door. There, I told you the car would fit! It only cost about $400 to fix the wall.

Rose only needed about an hour to stop laughing. Thank goodness she took it that way—it could have been a terrible evening.

Characters and High Jinks

Anne Goss gave me a great anecdote about her husband Bailey, when he was trying to ease the pain of a sizable hangover following a night on the town. He was nursing a Bloody Mary when Anne came into the kitchen and said their daughter Rochelle was having trouble saddling her horse.

Bailey groused that that was something Rochelle would have to learn to do if she wanted to learn to ride. But Anne persisted and Bailey went to the stable to lend a hand.

The horse kept rearing everytime Bailey tried to grab the reins. After several tries, he snatched the reins and then threw the best punch he could muster, aimed at the soft tissue around the animal's nose. But he missed by a couple inches and smacked the solid bone area, causing a great deal of pain—for Bailey. His hand puffed up and his arm in a sling, he missed playing golf for a couple of weeks. The punch-a-horse technique was later perfected by Alex Karras in the movie *Blazing Saddles*.

While on the subject of animal stories, I recall an incident that happened on a trip to California with the Colts when the team spent a few days at a Palo Alto hotel while preparing for a game against the San Francisco 49ers. Each day would end with a burger-beer affair attended by all the players and coaches.

In a room adjacent to the main dining room was a huge fish tank, maybe four feet deep. I wandered into the room some five minutes after the burger-bash adjourned one night to see defensive tackle Eugene "Big Daddy" Lipscomb with an arm in the tank, trying to catch a fish the hard way.

While "Big Daddy" was still flailing away, in walked quarterback John Unitas. After a brief discussion to determine what the problem was, John resolutely put an arm into the tank and landed a fish on the *first try*.

"How'd you do that?" asked an incredulous Lipscomb.

"It's easy," said the team leader. "All you have to do is know the pass route."

On occasion, humor surfaces in the strangest places: like at a morgue, for instance.

When "Big Daddy" succumbed to a drug overdose in 1963, his teammates were stunned. They knew the huge defensive tackle of the Colts drank alcohol, but drugs seemed an unlikely possibility. Needle marks were found in his right arm, and since "Big Daddy" was right-handed that seemed more than a little strange. But he was gone.

Trainer Bill Neill and team doctor Erwin Mayer were called to the morgue to make positive identification. Mayer was a very dignified, quiet gentleman who wore rimless spectacles and was always impeccably attired in three-piece suits. With that image, what was to come out of his mouth was startling.

When the morgue attendant pulled out the tray and took the sheet off the nude body, Neill and Mayer agreed that it was indeed "Big Daddy."

Lipscomb was a huge man in all departments and there he was with all his maleness exposed. Mayer nudged Neill and said, "I've got one just like that."

"You mean to tell me you've got one just as big?"

"No—just as dead!"

Chapter 13

My Partners and Others in the Booth

I was fortunate enough to have shared the microphone with a select few men who were elected to the Broadcasters' Wing at the Baseball Hall of Fame.

The list started with Byrum Saam, one of my broadcast partners during my first major league baseball assignment in Philadelphia, and continued with Bob Wolff in Washington and Ernie Harwell in Baltimore.

If I had a vote, I would also include the late Bill O'Donnell as being worthy of a plaque in Cooperstown, and it goes without saying that Jon Miller, currently the main voice of the Orioles who also does ESPN "Sunday Night Baseball," will eventually be enshrined. That's a given.

Perhaps it helps to have a great voice, but not all the guys in the Hall of Fame fit that mode. Russ Hodges did not have a great voice, Red Barber had a unique style, and Mel Allen had a distinctive voice. Not all had a voice that would qualify as a mellifluous vehicle, but they were awfully good at what they did.

Saam had a Texas twang, but his voice was easy to listen to and it was recognized immediately. I guess that would be one of the things that sponsors look for—immediate recognition of the broadcaster. Winning teams might help a broadcaster gain recognition, but consider Saam—he *never* covered a winner!

Ain't the Beer Cold!

I spent 16 years with the late Bill O'Donnell in Baltimore, my longest stretch with any partner. It was a wonderful association and I had a tremendous amount of respect for his professional ability.

Bill was accepted exceptionally well in Baltimore and he was held in high esteem at his previous job in Syracuse, where he broadcast football games for the Orangemen when they were a college power. While there, Bill was invited by coach Ben Schwartzwalder to give a pre-game pep talk to the Orangemen. They had to respect him immensely to extend such a rare honor. If that has happened to another broadcaster, it has escaped my attention.

Bill underwent cancer surgery in 1981, and made enough progress to return to work. But a year later, he had another operation and never fully recovered. Sometime after the second operation, he wanted to come back to the booth and do his share.

That sounded like a great idea if he could do it, but I wasn't sure it was going to help. In retrospect, I think Bill knew that there was only one way the story would end—he wanted to sit in that chair and talk baseball with the Baltimore fans *one more time*.

The night he returned, we went in to an extended rain delay. As long as I live, I'll remember Bill stretched across three metal chairs in the back of the booth during the delay, trying to conserve as much energy as possible for the resumption of the game. I begged him to go home. But professionals don't quit—and Bill completed the game. That was his only comeback attempt and he died October 29, 1982.

I hope that sometime, somehow, that those who have the say in Cooperstown will remember that Bill O'Donnell belongs there.

As partners, Bill and I worked out a deal with the Orioles whereby we'd each get a few days off around the All-Star Game and have a kind of vacation. We appreciated the Orioles agreeing to such an arrangement.

I had a difficult time accepting Bill's death, but one of the blackest days of my career came in 1962, when I was awakened by a telephone call one morning in Minneapolis and given the news that Bailey Goss had been fatally injured in a traffic accident while driving home the previous night following a Colts' party at the Belvedere Hotel.

I had known Bailey since our days in Reading and after I was hired by the National Brewing Co., I did the Orioles play-by-play in 1955 and 1956 and Bailey handled the commercials. There was no one better doing a commercial. When you mentioned Goss, you automatically thought beer. Many people said that when he talked about National Beer, it was difficult to stay away from the refrigerator.

Bailey had trouble staying awake in an airplane—he'd just adjust the seat belt, lean back, and he'd be gone. He even used to doze at Orioles games in Memorial Stadium. Soon after he did a commercial, I'd look over and he would have his face down on his fist, away in slumberland.

That didn't bother me, actually, but fans in the mezzanine level would start hollering, "Wake him up, Chuck—don't let him do that." I'd bump Bailey under the table without much success. Finally, I'd cut the microphone and say, "Hey, they're hollering at you for sleeping."

"Who's sleeping?"

"You are."

"Oh."

I think part of the problem was that there was not enough action for him in baseball. Now football was different; he was in the game right up to his ears. He knew the game well and the Philadelphia Eagles were interested in him, I think, as an offensive lineman out of Albright College. But with his good looks, great voice, and wonderful presence, Bailey did the right thing and went into broadcasting.

Dozing in the Memorial Stadium broadcast booth or while traveling in a plane was acceptable. But dozing at the wheel of an automobile was an entirely different matter. He did that the last time we went anywhere when he drove—went through a red light at an intersection and lightly tapped the car ahead.

I drove us home that night and thereafter, every time we went somewhere together, I was the designated driver. On the night of the fatal crash, he was driving alone when he rammed the back of a truck near Northern Parkway and Falls Road. I couldn't help thinking that if I had been there, I would have been driving and Bailey wouldn't have met a premature death.

He was a Baltimore legend in the early days of television, held in high esteem as were Jerry Turner and Al Sanders in later years. All three were honored by massive public turnouts for their respective funerals.

I found it hard to concentrate when I broadcast the game on the night after learning of Bailey's death. But it was better than sitting in a hotel room wondering why such tragedies happen.

I got through the game, but then the brewery asked me to do what I consider the most difficult task I had ever been assigned in broadcasting. They asked me to fly to California immediately and put my voice on the soundtracks that had featured Bailey, so that the commercials could continue until the brewery and the advertising agency could develop a better plan.

I boarded the plane for California with a heavy heart and Vikings football coach Norm Van Brocklin, who was aboard, apparently felt the depth of my misery. He sat down next to me in the first-class section and started to sketch plays and talk football.

He just forced me to listen. He didn't want me to sit and brood, to feel sorry for myself, as had been the case during the day and through the game. I'll never forget that flight, what Van tried to do for me. He may have been a very volatile man, but in his heart he was very considerate and caring as he tried to help me get over something that took me a long time to shake. As we parted in Los Angeles, the "Dutchman" said something I'll never forget: "You're a pro—do your job."

After Bailey's death, I missed him so much it wasn't much fun for me, on or off the job. I quit playing golf for about 10 years because everytime I went to a golf course it brought back memories because Bailey wasn't there anymore. I just said to myself, "It's no damned fun and I'm not going to play."

So I started going fishing at Loch Raven Reservoir, later

bought a boat and kept it there, and met a lot of great friends who loved that area and helped me become a bass fisherman. I fell for the sport, you might say, hook, line, and sinker.

An elderly gentleman, Red Slaysman, took me under his wing. He knew a lot more than others about the bottom of the reservoir, having hunted coon in the area before it was flooded to form the reservoir. It took me a couple years before I learned how to catch fish out there.

I think bass fishing is just great because they are so hard to figure. They don't have any particular behavioral patterns—they don't always bite when the sun goes down or comes up, or when the wind is from a certain direction, and they take a lot of different kind of bait.

The biggest bass I ever took out of Loch Raven was caught when the temperature was about 96 and there was not even a ripple on the water. We weighed it at seven and a half pounds, took pictures of my catch, and placed the fish in a holding pen. My idea was to put it back in the water after it recovered from the shock of being caught, to give someone else a chance at landing such a magnificent prize. But the fish died before I was able to release it.

A group of guys that I had gotten to know decided that we would tag and release all our catches, and it got to be a great game. After landing the fish, you'd look to find a friend's tag, then go and tell him where you made the catch. It was a nice experience.

It was only poetic justice, I guess, that a guy named Johnny Bass lured me back to the golf course. Johnny was a golf pro who started at the municipal course at Clifton Park and moved to Pine Ridge when it opened in 1959, not far from my favorite fishing spot.

He was upset about me giving up the game, kept urging me to come back, and finally convinced me to ride with him as he played a round. Next thing I knew, I began hitting a few shots and not long after that, I was back on the course.

For recreation and good times, I'd have to say that bass fishing and golf have been two of the most pleasurable hobbies of my life. I've met a lot of great people and spent many enjoyable moments on the water and on the course.

Getting back to my thoughts on broadcasting. The voices may sound different and the approaches to play-by-play may vary, but the one constant for all those in the booth is preparation.

One of the most meticulous in that respect was Bob Wolff. Like Bill O'Donnell, he was an outstanding student in school and each had an undying love of baseball.

Bob was a little more outgoing of the two. When we traveled with the Senators, we would mingle with the players and coaches. The Senators weren't supposed to win very often, and they didn't. But even with a losing team, darn we had fun.

Bob would bring a ukulele on the airplane and four or five of the players would join us in a singalong. Jim Lemon would be in there, and so would Roy Sievers. It was a delightful way to spend the travel time. What would happen if you tried that today? I have to laugh when I think about that possibility.

Bob Wolff's grammar was perfect, but he wasn't above stepping out of character with a word or phrase if he thought it would help him make a point. And, he had what all good broadcasters in my lifetime have had, the ability to prepare for the job at hand.

We alternated radio and television from game to game, and in Washington's Griffith Stadium you had to go past the radio booth to reach the TV location. One day when Bob was to be on television, he came by before the game with his wife, Jane, and a guy who served as a runner and another woman, probably a friend of his wife.

He waved a hello as he went past and I heard him say to his wife, "It's there, I know it's there, because I put it there." At first I didn't know what he meant, but I soon found out.

Bob was going on TV and he was wearing a button-down shirt with one button missing. He had the button in his hand and what he had "put there" were a needle and thread. The button was sewed on, and he went on camera properly dressed. That, I suggest, is preparation.

Bill O'Donnell exhibited the same kind of attention to detail

My Partners and Others in the Booth

in much different circumstances. After we did an afternoon game on the road and we were cleaning up, putting things away in our attache cases, Bill would pull out an index book from his pocket.

In it he'd have listed under the various cities, some six to eight restaurants, their phone numbers and locations, and even the names of the maitre d' in many cases. We'd meet traveling secretary Phil Itzoe and others after the game and go to the restaurant that had been chosen by "committee" vote, secure in the knowledge provided by O'Donnell.

Frank Messer came to Baltimore out of Richmond, Virginia, a true southern gentleman with a good sense of humor who knew his job in-and-out and was thoroughly prepared everytime he sat down at the microphone. He and O'Donnell overlapped two years in Baltimore before Frank left to join the Yankees' broadcast team.

I told Frank he would be a fool not to take the job in New York. But I gave him the same advice I had given Jim West when he went to broadcast hockey in Chicago: "You can do it but there's one thing you must be sure of—you're going into one of leading markets in the world, so make them pay for it." I hope Jim and Frank were paid handsomely for their talents.

While he was working the Orioles' games, Frank pulled a pretty good practical joke on me during a trip to Kansas City when they had a natural grass field that was well manicured by the skilled George Toma. But as good as the playing surface was, conditions were just the opposite in the broadcast booth and the press lounge.

We should have been eligible for hazardous pay in the booth, where you could walk into steel girders if you were more than five feet tall. In those days, before intercoms, we had to head for the press box if we needed information and didn't mind risking personal injury if you were in a hurry.

These days, the press lounge in Kansas City may be the best in all of baseball. But in those early years, they served the worst hamburgers I ever tasted. That's all they served—hamburgers, hot dogs, and soda—and after tasting the burgers, you dared not try the hot dogs.

Ain't the Beer Cold!

Anyway, between games of a doubleheader one day, we stayed on the air instead of returning the signal to the studio. Frank got the lineups and I did the sign-on and the first couple innings. After the game started, Frank said he had to get something to eat at a concession stand. I reminded him that the concession food was as bad as that in the press lounge. But Frank said he was starving and left the booth.

He returned with a soda and two burgers wrapped in tin foil, rubbed his hands as if anticipating a feast, unwrapped one of the tin foils...and exposed a burger with a bite taken out of it!!

We took one look and lost control, laughing our silly heads off while the game was in progress. I finally figured out that Messer had set me up by taking the bite from the burger and then rewrapping it, so he could break me up on the air.

After he went to work in New York, Frank told me of some delightful repartee that occurred during a Yankee broadcast.

Broadcaster Bill White had to leave the booth temporarily and asked his partner Phil Rizzuto to mark his scorecard during his absence. When he returned, Bill understood such notations as "6-3" or "K" and the normal descriptions of the plays that had occurred, but the one that had him stumped was where "Scooter" had wrtitten "W.W." next to the batter's name.

"What's W.W.?" Bill asked. "What does that stand for?"

Little Phil had a ready and, to him , a quite logical response: *Wasn't watching.*"

Ernie Harwell was the kind of broadcaster that all others in the business admire tremendously because of his ability to describe the action no matter what happened after the pitch was made. It was uncanny; as if he had a sixth sense to know what was going to happen when the ball was hit.

The thing that I admired most about Ernie was that no matter what happened on the field, he was always in control. All of us who have heard him can be grateful that we were exposed to one of baseball's great broadcasters.

In my opinion Vin Scully has always been the No. 1 man in the game, a true wordsmith who is gramatically correct in every-

My Partners and Others in the Booth

thing he says and never loses control no matter what transpires on the field. The words he uses so effortlessly I have a helluva time finding when I'm in the booth.

The day that Hall-of-Fame pitcher Don Drysdale died unexpectedly, Vin proved again that he was a consummate pro. Drysdale died just before gametime, but his wife was out with the children and had not yet been notified.

So nothing was said of his death during the broadcast and the listening audience never knew that Scully had lost his broadcasting partner and one of his best friends. He performed his job the way Dodgers fans had expected over the years—brilliantly.

Brooks Robinson became a delightful companion in the TV booth as an analyst after ending his Hall-of-Fame playing career in 1977. I learned a lot from Brooksie in 1983, the year he was enshrined at Cooperstown. I had a few interviews in my induction year, but nothing compared with the media onslaught on the former third baseman. There were radio and TV interviews in every city on the road, and I never heard him complain.

I thought by July he'd turn to me and say, "Boy, I'll be glad when this is over, Charley." But he never did; he never once found fault with the incessant requests.

One thing I learned from Brooks was his understanding and compassion for people, as he exhibited when we were broadcasting one day, I think in Detroit.

With the game in progress, a little boy stood up on ground level behind the box seats and held up a program to indicate he would like to have an autograph. Brooks held up one finger as if to say, "wait a minute."

As soon as the inning ended and we started to roll a commercial, Brooks left the booth, ran downstairs, signed the autograph, and returned without missing a play.

I've been present when fans asked for autographs and Brooks would engage them in conversation. He'd ask where they were from, where they went to school, and why they were fans of the Orioles. The fans could feel he was genuine in his concern and were honored by such attention. His wife Connie, who was a

153

flight attendant on an Orioles' charter when they met, acts the same way with strangers.

The only suggestion I ever made to Brooks of a serious nature was that when his kids grew up and left the house, that he should take Connie with him whenever possible. I failed to do that with my wife, and I paid dearly. Rose became a cancer victim and spent too many hours alone when I should have been there with her. Brooks took my advice.

On the air, Brooks enjoyed what he was doing, but I got the feeling that he was thinking, "Doggone it, I wish I was out there doing it instead of sitting here watching."

He had tremendous respect for Clete Boyer of the Yankees, saying he was the best third baseman he'd ever seen. He really didn't talk in depth about the kind of stuff a pitcher had. I got the feeling that Brooks really didn't care as a player; if he could hit the pitch, he would.

As a player, Brooks had a habit of fleeing the clubhouse as soon as possible after the game ended. But he was very cooperative with the media—if they were there before he was ready to leave.

In Baltimore, if the final out was a flyball to the outfield, Brooks would check to make sure the ball would be caught, then turn and run toward the dugout. He'd shed his uniform jersey before reaching the clubhouse, where he would take off the rest of his clothes, shower, jump into a T-shirt and slacks, and be gone within five minutes of the final out.

Away from the field, he was just as impatient. Brooks was a rapid eater and his body battery never needed recharging because it never ran down. One night in New York, I was in a group that went out for a post-game beer or two.

About five or 10 minutes after the beers were delivered at our first stop, Brooks said, "OK, let's go." So we went to a couple other places and repeated the process over and over.

A friend told me that one night, he and two or three others went out with Brooks and did the same "sip-and-leave" routine. Their fifth stop turned out to be the same establishment where they had started the bar hopping about 90 minutes earlier.

My Partners and Others in the Booth

Brooks was so good-natured that when he was the butt of a joke he'd laugh harder than anyone, so I developed a devious plan one day. I had a pair of binoculars used for viewing the bullpen action and other things in the crowd that could be more interesting.

I knew that Brooks used my binoculars more than I did, so I coated the lens with the eye-black that players smear under their eyes to soften the glare from the sun or lights. Then I put them on the table near the microphone and waited.

I figured it would only take about a half inning before Brooks picked them up and he would have a ring around his eyes, the way Colonel Potter did when Corporal Radar pulled the same stunt on the TV hit show, "*M*A*S*H*."

But no such luck. He didn't touch those binoculars all through the game, and I later found out that he had been warned by trainer Ralph Salvon, who had supplied me with the eye-black. I learned a lesson: It doesn't pay to involve a good friend of the intended victim in the plot.

I only worked with Bill Veeck, and sometimes with Al Rosen, in the early '60s on the NBC "Game of the Week," when the National Brewing Co. sponsored the game in an area that reached down into the Carolinas. We would do the first half of the games with the National Brewing Co. commercials while using the network video feed of the game, then our audience would hear the network announcers for the remainder of the game.

The network games were on Saturday afternoons. I'd arrive at the site of the game on Friday and go to bed somewhere about midnight. About 1:30 or so, the telephone would ring and Veeck would be on the other end with the same message everytime: "Charles, it's the shank of the evening. Let's go!"

So I'd get dressed, go to the lobby and meet Bill. He could find a place in every city to drink beer and talk baseball, no matter what the time. One night in Detroit we wound up in a house of ill repute, where the den looked as good as any cocktail lounge I'd ever seen. We drank beer and talked baseball (honest) until Bill sent me back to the hotel in a cab. About 10:30 the next morning, I was on my way to the ballpark when I encountered Bill coming back from his night on the town.

155

Ain't the Beer Cold!

Veeck was a good analyst because of his extensive knowledge about baseball. When he ran the Chicago White Sox, he tried to end those automatic outs at second base on double play relays by placing cameras along the first- and third-base lines to record what he referred to as "proximity plays." The word got around to the umpires and pretty soon they made certain that the force plays at second base in Comiskey Park were actually made.

Bill rarely referred to Brooks Robinson simply as Brooks. He felt that everything that was good about baseball was wrapped up in "Mr. Robinson." First, was his ability and secondly, his infectious attitude toward the game. Brooks loved the game and had a helluva good time playing. He couldn't wait to get out on the field (and, as I noted earlier, he couldn't wait to leave, either).

Brooks showed the same intensity after the Orioles defeated the Chicago White Sox, 3-0, to win the American League Championship Series on October 8, 1983 at Comiskey Park.

While the celebration continued in the clubhouse, Brooks and I, along with TV director Sheldon Shemer, headed for the bus to await the remainder of the traveling party. After a couple more guys appeared, someone said he would like to have a beer.

Brooks, impatient as always, jumped up and said, "Who wants a beer?" and added, "OK, got you covered" after getting several orders. About five minutes later he was back with a cold six-pack. As talk of the Series continued, it didn't take long to finish the beer.

Shemer yelled, "Hey, No. 5, we're empty." Brooks jumped off the bus and located another six-pack. I got to thinking that not many people have been served by perhaps the greatest fielding third baseman in the history of the game.

Something happened in the 10th inning of that final ALCS game that made a lasting impression on me. After Chicago's Britt Burns had given up a solo homer to Tito Landrum of the Orioles, which snapped a scoreless tie, the White Sox lefty was relieved.

As we rolled to a commercial, as we usually do during pitching changes, I saw Burns turn over the ball to manager Tony LaRussa and head toward the dugout.

My Partners and Others in the Booth

As Burns departed, four or five Orioles, led by Rick Dempsey, stood on the top step of the dugout and applauded his gallant effort. Burns casually turned his head slightly in the direction of the Orioles and softly touched the peak of his cap, as if to say, "Thank you."

I don't recall seeing that too often, and it was a moment to remember.

Before ending my thoughts about the broadcast booth, let me bring up a few gems from out of the past:

Bob Elson, broadcasting a game pitched by Saul Rogovin, who couldn't throw hard enough to break a pane of glass: "Rogovin winds and fires—we pause for station identification, this is the Chicago White Sox network—ball, low and outside."

Another from Elson: "There's a flyball deep into left field—got a lovely wire from Fifi and the girls at the Riptide—and it's in there for a home run."

Bob Prince before the Pirates muffed a ninth-inning rally: "The Buccos have got 'em right where they want 'em—tying run at second base, two down in the bottom of the ninth. Here's the pitch—see you tomorrow night, same time, same station."

Jerry Coleman, the Yankees second baseman who was famous for his malaprops:

"...swings and misses, and it's a foul back off the screen."

"They threw Winfield out at second—and he's safe."

"...steals second base standing up—he slid when he didn't have to."

While giving scores: "Kansas City at Chicago, or Chicago at Kansas City—doesn't make any difference—Kansas City *leads in the eighth, 4-4.*"

Anonymous football broadcaster: "Stay tuned for another exciting afternoon of 'Countdown to Kissoff.'"

The public address announcer at the College All-Star Game, who introduced the Colts' quarterback as "John Unit-ass," driving general manager Don Kellett through the press box roof.

From outside the press box, let me relay something I heard from the great newscaster Lowell Thomas one night while driving home from Philadelphia to Reading. Thomas used to end his newscast with a "kicker" before Hugh James came in for a final word.

On this night, Thomas told of a couple suing a veterinarian who, while treating a dog, had accidentally snipped off a piece of his tail. The unhappy couple said it had ruined the pet's appearance and sued for $25,000.

Then Thomas concluded with: "And Hugh, isn't that a lot to do about a little piece of tail?"

Hugh James never said a word, but when they hit the button to activate his microphone, he was laughing like crazy. After a few more seconds of silence, all that was heard was the familiar NBC chimes and the station identification:
"Bong...Bong...Bong...KYW, Philadelphia."

I nearly lost control of my car.

Chapter 14

Having a Ball at Work and Play

If there's one cardinal rule about working for a living, it should be to find something that you enjoy doing...to get some pleasure as well as a paycheck out of your chosen profession.

It helps immensely if those in authority feel the same way and encourage the feeling of pleasure on the job. And, that was exactly the atmosphere around the National Brewing Co., which I proudly represented for 23 years.

Jerome (Jerry) DiPaolo, the brewery's Maryland sales manager thought highly of a young man he wanted to hire as a salesman and when the interview was about to start, he wondered if the potential employee had a sense of humor. So he asked assistant advertising manager Bill Costello to lend a helping hand.

While DiPaolo was conducting the interview, Costello called on the intercom, "Jerome, I'd like to see you."

"I've got someone in the office—I'll get back to you."

Another minute, another interruption and the same message from DiPaolo: "I already told you, I have someone in the office and I can't talk now. Soon as I'm finished, I'll be right down, OK?"

A few moments passed and on the intercom Bill said, "Jerome, when are you coming over?"

Ain't the Beer Cold!

"Bill, how many times have I got to tell you? I have someone in the office and as soon as I'm free, I'll let you know."

Then Jerry turned to the young man and said, "That's one of the things you'll have to learn to live with if you come to work here. You'll have to learn to put up with an S.O.B. like that. He gets me so mad, I want to kill him some days."

Then, Bill interrupted once more, "Jerry, I've waited long enough—we've got to talk."

"Damn it, excuse me," Jerry said as he opened a desk drawer, whipped out a stage gun loaded with blanks, ran down the hall to the adjacent office, and fired—BANG, BANG, BANG! Bill screamed and fell from his chair.

"Well," Bill said as he got off the floor, "do you think he has a sense of humor?"

"I don't know, let's find out." They walked back to Jerry's office, and his secretary reported that the young man had fled the premises! Yes, the National Brewing Co. was a wonderful place to work in those days.

I recall the day we introduced Washington broadcaster John McClean to the Baltimore media at Skip Meushaw's restaurant on the beltway on a day which coincided with the birthday of National Brewing Vice President Pat Roche.

Jerry DiPaolo said we couldn't let that pass unnoticed, so he asked Skip to place little birthday candles in each order of crab imperial. Then when Jerry came up the line lighting the candles, he skipped John's, lit mine and Pat's, then headed back to John's place setting. Somehow, I got an urgent message to head for safer ground, so I pushed my chair back, and got up in a hurry.

"Where are you going?" Pat said.

"I've got to go to the john," I said, and had only taken about two steps when—BLAM—there was an explosion from a fire cracker that sent crab imperial to the ceiling and all over McClean and Roche. Meushaw was furious and made DiPaolo clean the crab off the ceiling.

The brewery held a sales meeting at an Ocean City restaurant one afternoon and we were so exhuberant that we were politely

Having a Ball at Work and Play

asked to leave before regular customers began to arrive for the dinner hour. Jerry DiPaolo paid the bill, but we couldn't find John Schneider, the marketing director who was miffed by the not-too-subtle bum's rush.

Jerry retreated into a little corridor and spotted John surveying the room, as if looking for something. "Hey, John, let's go," said Jerry.

"Be right with you."

Jerry said again it was time to go as John said, "Ah, there it is," pulled the main electrical switch wich plunged the restaurant into darkness, and then added, "Now—let's go!"

Bailey Goss and I had lots of laughs on the job, sometimes while the sporting event was in progress. Bailey used to describe wrestling on television, and one night he insisted that I accompany him to see champion Antonio Rocca at the Coliseum on Monroe Street in Baltimore. I really didn't want to go because I didn't consider wrestling athletic competition, but more of an entertainment show. Still, I was able to appreciate the athletic feats of such huge men, so I tagged along.

At the Coliseum, I was pretending to enjoy the feature match involving Rocca, when I noticed that Bailey kept moving his chair back from the table next to the ring apron. When he continued to edge back, I figured something was up. I thought, if he's going to move, so am I. But instead of moving back, I moved laterally away from Bailey.

No sooner had I moved, than Rocca tossed his opponent from the ring, directly into the seat I had vacated. Bailey, who had devised the plan with Rocca's help, howled with laughter, but was disappointed over the outcome and wondered why I had left the premises. I told him, "I didn't think you were moving for no reason at all." Rocca was on target with his toss, but didn't hit the bull's-eye (me) because of my quick departure. The tossee bounced off the ring apron before hitting the chair, and wasn't injured. As usual, he was the perfect foil.

The love of laughter extended all the way to the top and included Jerold C. Hoffberger, the National Brewing Co.'s president who also became the president of the Orioles after the family-owned brewery became the team's majority owner in 1965. His credo with the ballclub was the same as that at the brewery: lead with confidence and enthusiasm—if you act like a winner, you'll be a winner; show me a good loser and I'll show you a consistent loser.

Hoffberger, who had been on the Orioles' board of directors previously, was named elected chairman of the board in June 1965 and in little over a year he was celebrating Baltimore's first modern-day baseball championship (the Orioles had been three-time champs of the National League in the 1890s).

He attended the 1966 World Series as a rookie owner when the Orioles faced the venerable Los Angeles Dodgers, and immediately encountered a ticket problem for the Series opener in Los Angeles.

Dodgers' boss Walter O'Malley had provided Hoffberger with 10 seats near the right-field foul pole, hardly a prime spot for the visiting owner's party. After the Orioles complained, the seats were relocated near the team dugout, but now there were only nine seats available—one shy of Hoffberger's needs.

Hoffberger realized the spot the Dodgers were in and didn't blame them for the mixup but, instead, offered a solution. Since he was carrying three cameras, with the straps around his neck, Jerry said he would *stand* in the spot allocated for photographers on the field level near one of the dugouts. But first, he had to convince the real photographers of his true identity by showing them his photo in the game program. For the second game, the working photographers brought him a box lunch from the media room.

"I bet no other owner had stood for two games of the World Series," Hoffberger said. "I had a great view—I only had to dodge a few foul balls."

As you can tell, there was a lot of camaraderie on the job at National and it extended into the friendships I developed with members of the media, representatives of the sponsors, and advertising media personnel.

To this day, I talk with many friends at least once a week by phone or in person, and take trips with some of them. Friendships

Having a Ball at Work and Play

mean a great deal to me and it's always fun recalling tales of our past accomplishments and/or embarrassments.

It certainly helps if they have a sense of humor—and the ability to play golf is an added bonus.

As we get older, we must realize that we'll lose some of our friends along the way. One who died in 1995 was Clifton Van Roby, a former basketball official, who also had a radio show in his native Cumberland, Maryland. He was one of the better golfers in my circle, having won several club championships and being credited with four holes-in-one.

Van could be referred to as a natty dresser and his color combinations at times bordered on the outrageous. As soon as he entered the clubhouse, Orioles pitcher Dave McNally would yell, "I'll give a dollar to anyone who can name a color he's NOT wearing."

Van went through life with a smile and had a good sense of humor. He loved the Orioles and on every trip to Baltimore he brought along a recorder to tape interviews for his show.

Coaches George Bamberger and Jim Frey would cooperate fully for taped interviews but invariably, after answering a few questions, the interviewees would let loose a tirade of expletives—and another tape would be ruined.

Pitcher Dave Leonhard, one of the most congenial of players, an erudite former student at Johns Hopkins University who was rather quiet, once started screaming in a vulgar fashion at the top of his lungs. I asked Dave what he was doing and he said simply, "Just fouling up the tapes."

Van was nicknamed "Homer" because of his alleged tendency as a basketball referee to call fouls which favored the home team. He loved the moniker.

Keith McBee, a television personality, passed away many years ago, but I still remember the evening I volunteered to drive him home from a Christmas party after he had already fallen asleep from overindulging. I was warned that if he were startled, he might react in an unfriendly manner, particularly if he didn't recognize the person with him.

I kept a careful eye on Keith as he slept with his head resting against the side window of my car. He opened his left eye and stared at me. "Hey, Mac, how you doing?" I asked.

I don't know if he recognized me or if it was the state or mind he was in, but he took a long look and said simply, "Scoobi, doobie, doo." Then he went back to sleep.

When I arrived somewhere in the area of his home, I went into a police station to get specific directions. The cops said they'd take care of Keith, but two of them weren't exactly sure of his address. A third officer intervened and said he'd try to get the information.

He left the room to talk with Keith and returned in about a half minute. "I don't know what's going on," said the officer. "All he said was, 'scoobie, doobie, doo.'"

The police escorted Keith to his home, carried him in, and placed him on the sofa. His wife, used to such arrangements, said, "Chuck, where do you think I ought to start looking for the car?"

"All I know is that he went to a party at Monumental Films," I replied. "Maybe you ought to take a peek around there."

McBee was one of the most solid newscasters in the Baltimore area and was so highly regarded that ABC used him on Saturday night network newscasts. He was a great storyteller who was beloved by all in the business and when he got out of sorts it was as much our fault as his, because we'd buy him a few drinks to hear a few more stories.

Walter "Bud" Freeman is another friend who plays golf and has a good sense of humor. It's a delight to be in the company of Bud, an accomplished after-dinner speaker who once worked in marketing and public relations for the Orioles.

Bud was in my kitchen one night, along with Cliff Van Roby, and Suter Kegg, former sports editor of the *Cumberland* (MD) *Times*. Bud was sitting on the left of Suter and to Bud's left was Van.

As Bud was telling a story, he looked to his right and said, "Van..." Suter responded, "My name is Suter."

Bud continued with his story, again addressed Suter with the incorrect name and again got the same response: *"My name is Suter."* We all got to laughing and crying at the same time.

Having a Ball at Work and Play

When Bud made the same mistake again, he added: "I know—your name is Suter." Then he asked me for a paper napkin, on which he wrote "Suter" in two-inch letters, punched a hole in the napkin, and hung it from Suter's left ear to give him fair warning the next time he turned that way.

Bud and I were in a foursome one day on the Hunt Valley golf course, where the eighth hole was next to a magnificent house surrounded by a rail fence. One of our foursome hit a drive into the backyard where two Labrador retrievers were sitting.

The other guy said they look like friendly dogs and suggested someone should go in and get the ball.

"How do you know they're friendly?" Bud said.

"Look at them...they're playing with a frisbee."

"That's not a frisbee," Bud deadpanned. "That's what's left of the gas man."

Chick Serio, still another golfing friend, is a vitamin freak. He digests them all day; it's become a way of life. In the middle of the day, he finds it necessary to eat something with the vitamins.

One day we were playing a round of golf at Rocky Point, when Chick went into the snack bar to get some peanut butter crackers and a soda to go with the vitamins. He chomped on the crackers as we played the 10th hole, and he was first off the tee on number 11. While hitting the tee shot, a squirrel made off with Chick's vial of pills, ignoring the crackers in the golf cart.

John Lazell, the club pro, called Chick the next morning and said, "I don't ever want to see you again."

"Why? What's the matter?"

"Already this morning, I've had three squirrels call for starting times."

Chapter 15

Baseball Then, Now, and Later

Looking back on my long career as a broadcaster in Baltimore, I'd have to say that I was very fortunate to be around during the glory years of both the Colts and the Orioles.

I've talked to three or four generations of fans in parts of six decades (the '40s to the '90s) since beginning with the International League Orioles in 1949. I know that some of my early listeners must now be great-grandparents, because I'm one myself.

When I started to broadcast, defensive players left their gloves on the baseball field when they went on offense and there were only 16 teams instead of the current 28 in the major leagues.

It's still 60 feet, six inches from the pitching rubber to the plate, but some things have changed. We now have exploding scoreboards and expanded coverage with video boards that offer fans message space and televised replays.

There's been a tremendous increase in the number of reporters and sportscasters covering the game, and a good number of women are now in the business.

Complaints like the length of the games and the dimensions of the strike zone are still around, as they have been for years. And arguments persist over the use of designated hitters and the

Baseball Then, Now, and Later

possibility of interleague play. But don't expect any sudden changes; staid old baseball usually moves at a glacier pace.

I was told by Billy Hunter, the former Orioles' shortstop and coach, how difficult it was to have the league even consider changing the way checked swings were called. He thought the homeplate umpire could sometimes be blocked from seeing whether or not a batter had committed himself on a swing.

So, Billy suggested that the first-base umpire should be responsible for determining whether a right-handed batter had swung, and the third-base umpire for a left-handed batter. He once attended the umpires' winter meeting to promote the idea, talked to them throughout the various seasons, and even wrote letters to advance his checked-swing theory and also his idea to have umpires positioned on the infield side of second base to better call tag plays at that base. The ideas eventually were adopted, but only after many years of lobbying.

The designated hitter rule gives me a pain. I'm not against the DH, not at all, if it can keep a lot of aging good hitters active. My criticism is that if you have a DH, then everybody should have it—or nobody should have it. It doesn't seem fair that the DH can be used all season in the American League and then is barred from use in the World Series games at National League parks.

Most scoreboards were manually operated when I started in the business. Someone had to be behind the board to hang up the scores and pitchers' numbers. When I grew up, a fan had to have a program and he gave almost as much attention to the scoreboard as he did the game. Nowadays, fans can see replays of game action from parks all over the country, and computers handle messages, statistics, and quiz questions to keep the fans busy and, of course, most teams put the players' names on the backs of their uniforms.

There has been much moaning and groaning in recent years about the length of major league games. Some critics blame the radio and television commercials, but I suggest that it's the fault of the players and umpires.

I can't tell the number of times I've seen a pitcher go into his move, ready to pitch, when the umpire accedes to a hitter's request and calls time. Even when the pitcher has started his stride, the umpire may wave him off and yell, "No pitch—no pitch."

I think a batter must be made to stay in the box, at least with one foot. If he's not ready when the pitcher throws, well that's tough luck. You may remember that Cleveland manager Mike Hargrove was called "the human rain delay" because of his incessant routine of adjusting various pieces of equipment between pitches. At the start of my career, I once counted the number of times that Harry (The Hat) Walker touched his cap and his top mark between two pitches was 17!!

Another way to speed up the game considerably would be to have specialists who are strictly ball-and-strike umpires, just as there are middle relievers and closers, and batters who face only certain pitchers. Baseball is a game of specialists, so why not extend it to umpiring?

What bothers me is that with a four-man umpiring crew, the possibility exists that batters and pitchers could be looking at four different strike zones on consecutive days. I feel that if you were to ask every team to fill out a form to name the best ball-and-strike umpires, there would be a concensus on those at the top.

The late Bill Klem, a member of the Baseball Hall of Fame, once had a stretch of 16 consecutive years behind the plate. If a guy is good at that job, then reward him. There could be two such specialists in each crew, alternating every day. Then the players would have a better idea of the strike zone rather than have to go through an early-inning test in every game to determine its dimensions.

I'm also disturbed by the recent trend of hitters attacking pitchers after they've been hit by a pitch. My personal feeling is, that if you're going to play major league baseball, you'll have to expect being chased off the plate and sometimes struck. It's part of the game; always has been and always will be. Running out to the mound to inflict personal injury is not the way to respond.

Frank Robinson had the best response by bearing down a little harder and getting a decisive hit. Pretty soon the word got around: "Don't wake him up, let him alone; it's bad enough facing him when he's asleep."

Baseball Then, Now, and Later

Brooks Robinson was beaned seven times in his career, but he never charged the mound. He often said the only thing he ever charged was dinner for his wife.

The pitcher has a right to move the batter off the plate, the right to intimidate the batter if he can. Don Drysdale, Bob Gibson, and Early Wynn were masters of that craft and, it's worth noting, all were elected to the Baseball Hall of Fame.

John Logan, the former Milwaukee Braves' shortstop, told me a story about batting against Drysdale just after the previous hitter laced a double. "I hope he's not in a bad mood," Logan thought, "because if he is, I'm going to get it."

Logan got it all right, a fastball into the ribs. He went down on all fours, trying to catch his breath. "Did you say anything?" I asked.

"Oh, my God, no! I didn't say a word. I just got up and staggered down toward first."

"Did you look at him?"

"Oh no, I didn't look at him."

"What were you thinking?"

"Hot dog—0-for-4, instead of 0-for-5."

Former Orioles third baseman George Kell told of lining a single through the box against Early Wynn, who didn't take kindly to the smash past his ample torso. Wynn called time and summoned first baseman Al Rosen to the mound.

When he returned to the bag, Rosen started laughing and bent from the waist to hide his actions as best he could from the fans—and from Wynn, for that matter.

"What's so funny?" Kell asked.

"He wants to pick you off—and he wants to make sure I don't catch the ball."

Nothing further happened, but "Gus" was that kind of guy. I've often thought it was a shame that Wynn wasn't pitching the day that Bill Veeck sent Eddie Gaedel to bat as the leadoff hitter. I'm sure the little guy wouldn't have been shown any mercy by burly Early.

One of the greatest changes in sports in recent years has been the firm beachhead established by women in all phases of media coverage. You see them in dugouts, on the sidelines at football games, on call-in shows, and they do excellent work in studios. To my knowledge, women do everything in broadcasting except play-by-play, and there may be someone out there doing it already without my knowledge. There's no reason they can't.

It's obvious that those ladies who cast their lot with the media do their homework and are extremely well prepared. I congratulate them for doing something that for many years I thought would never happen. I'm happy that I was wrong—more power to them.

Athletes today are said to be bigger, stronger, and smarter than they were 20 years ago, and it probably could be proven. They also are much better paid. But the only thing that has grown faster than the salaries is the disabled list, which gets longer and longer every year. Interesting, don't you think?

Sometimes I wonder what effect escalating salaries will have on the game in the future. For instance, will millionaire players want to show up at fantasy camps for a mere pittance? Will old-timers' games disappear? If they do, it will be because the players really don't understand the feelings that fans have for them.

Many players look at fans as people who want autographs, nothing more. But there's much more to a fan that that. If you could come to my home and sit down to read the letters I received about my Hall-of-Fame induction, you'd understand that the fan is very, very special.

As much as the award meant to me and my family, the letters meant much more. They came from the elderly and young kids, from people I never heard of and many from out-of-state. Anytime you seek enlightenment about the true meaning of a fan, just check with me.

I learned a lot about players' attitudes when I broadcast Washington Senators games early in my career. Cookie Lavagetto was the manager and, as usual, things weren't going well for the Senators.

Cookie was upset one day when the Cleveland Indians were racking the pesky Nats pretty good. He strode up and down in the

Baseball Then, Now, and Later

dugout, kicking things as he paced. "I don't give a damn who it is, but the first batter up for them in the next inning had better go down, or it'll cost you $50," he said to his pitcher Tex Clevenger.

The first Indians' batter was Marty Keough, who just happened to be the godfather of Tex's son. Clevenger didn't throw at Marty and was fined the promised $50.

When we got back to Washington a week or so later, Tex summoned me to his clubhouse locker where he was catching up on his mail. He handed me a letter that was addressed to his son Marty, who was named after godfather Keough.

"Dear Marty," it read, "next time, tell your Daddy to do what he's supposed to do." It was signed by Keough, who also enclosed a $50 savings bond that made up for the fine.

I rate baseball the greatest game we have because the team ahead can't sit on the lead or run out the clock, and the trailing team always has its final turn at bat.

But I also think it's the attitude of people like Marty Keough who mean so much to the game. Maybe former pitcher Dan Quisenberry was right when he was asked what made baseball so great and he quipped: "No homework!"

Chapter 16

For the Love of the Game

Just call me a sentimental slob— my latent feelings have been fully exposed.

I was always aware that I had a soft spot in my heart for things nostalgic, but I didn't realize the depth of that feeling until I was overwhelmed with emotion at three ballpark events in the last few years.

The most recent was Cal Ripken's amazing run at the major league consecutive-game streak which culminated with an outdoor lovefest at Camden Yards on September 6, 1995. The post-game ceremony was televised nationally and evolved into a celebration that honored not only recordholder Cal, but all of baseball.

Previously, I was awash with sentiment (and tears) during the festive weekend surrounding the Orioles final game at venerable Memorial Stadium in 1991.

Even before the tasteful on-field celebration following the final game on October 6, 1991, I had already spilled my tear ducts two days earlier. Jon Miller was the master of ceremonies that night when Orioles broadcasters were honored, and I was asked to talk a little about my late broadcast partner, Bill O'Donnell.

I expected maybe a smattering of polite applause when I was introduced. But as I approached the microphone, the applause kept building and building. Then, when I looked around, the fans were

172

For the Love of the Game

actually standing! I tried to stop it by saying "thank you" several times—then I bowed—but nothing seemed to end the ovation. I didn't know what to do, and the cheering eventually died down.

I couldn't understand what was happening then and I still don't as I relate the anecdote for the book. I almost broke up completely and if I hadn't been able to concentrate and think about O'Donnell, I would have made a horse's *patoot* of myself, right in front of all those fans. I never had anything like that happen to me before.

I didn't think of it that night, but I remembered later, that I had watched my friend Ernie Harwell encounter the same emotion on the day he was honored at Tiger Stadium for his long and distinguished career as a broadcaster.

When I walked off the field, through the third-base dugout, and got to the runway, I lost whatever composure I had left. By the time I got to my car, I was sobbing like a baby. I've heard similar ovations for athletes and dignataries but never, ever expected anything like that to come my way. It was so unrehearsed and apparently so sincere—a great moment to experience such an outpouring from some of the same fans who helped pave my way to the Baseball Hall of Fame. Memories of that night will stay with me forever.

The celebration following the final Memorial Stadium game shifted the spotlight to the athletes, but I still had a few lumps in my throat. After all, this was the last game at a stadium where I had made my livelihood broadcasting football and baseball for 42 years.

Memorial Stadium, despite those huge concrete pillars that blocked the sight lines of so many fans, turned out to be a grand old ballpark—a home which housed the Orioles and the Colts, two of the most respected franchises in the histories of the major leagues and the National Football League.

So while I was a bit sentimental about losing an old friend, I also knew that a magnificent structure would open at Camden Yards the following season. The moment called for a special goodbye—and it was provided by the Orioles' marketing public

173

relations departments. The ensuing ceremony was absolutely brilliant.

After Cal Ripken grounded into a game-ending double play, the fans settled back to await what I think was the most magnificent pageant I've ever seen in a ballpark. Dr. Charles Steinberg, the director of public affairs, public relations director Rick Vaughn, and Julie Wagner, the director of community relations, headed a dedicated team which couldn't have done anything more to make the afternoon any more successful. It will go down as one of the greatest days in Orioles history, perhaps in the history of baseball.

The beauty was that it was accomplished without leaking any advance information to members of the media (where was Hugh Trader when we needed him? See Chapter 7). I never had an inkling what was in store, even when I happened to walk past former second baseman Bobby Grich on my way to the elevator and thought, "What's he doing here?" I saw a couple of other ex-players the previous day, but it didn't dawn on me that they were in town other than to watch a ballgame or visit friends.

Just before the game someone from the public relations staff came into the booth, handed us some papers, and said, "We know you're not going to say anything about this, but this is what we intend to do."

We were left with a list of all the ex-players, managers, and coaches who were expected to attend, and some 119 of them were on hand to share in the moment, which culminated when all those present formed a huge circle around the infield and waved goodbye to the fans.

One by one they had come out of the Orioles dugout, led by Baltimore's all-time favorite Brooks Robinson, and took their places at their familiar positions, wearing the type of Orioles uniform of the era in which each played. The haunting theme from the movie *Field of Dreams* was played over the public address system, making the scene even more surreal and the participants seem somewhat ghostlike as they jogged to their positions.

To have them announced, I feel, would have completely

For the Love of the Game

destroyed the desired effect. The fans didn't need to hear the names; they had seen them play in their prime, and it was nice to have them back home again.

The thing I remember most was the silence of the applause; it was as if the fans found it difficult to shout. It was something like a wake, where old friends come to say their goodbyes and share treasured memories. They wish they weren't there but since they were, it was time to quietly rejoice.

It was such an emotional moment that I suspect 90 percent of the crowd was choked up. That's the way it was in the broadcast booth. I had "walking pneumonia" that day and Jon Miller handled the lion's share of the work in his normally brilliant manner. After a while, he stopped naming each man as he came out, but just kind of gave some offhand recognition that each was there.

I looked through my field glasses at Brooks and, as I'd seen him do a thousand times, he bowed his head as he scratched the skin of the infield dirt with his spikes, and when he glanced toward homeplate he looked a bit misty-eyed.

Jim Palmer was next out and I could see the emotion building up as he stood at the pitcher's mound. I imagine if you could have gotten close to anyone on the field, you could have felt the emotional impact. More than a few have since commented that they, too, were crying.

I don't recall seeing any "high fives." Instead they shook hands with others at their positions and then either hugged one another or gave a friendly pat on the back.

Then homeplate was dug from its moorings by members of the grounds crew who were attired in white tuxedos with Oriole orange bow ties and cummerbunds. The plate was transported to Camden Yards, where its arrival was seen by the Memorial Stadium crowd on DiamondVision. Broadcaster Jim McKay, a Baltimore native, handled that part of the program with a grandson at his side, completing a terrific afternoon.

As I walked through thousands of people leaving the park, I didn't hear any cheers, only warm-hearted, meaningful applause. And, as I exited for the last time from Memorial Stadium as a

Ain't the Beer Cold!

broadcaster, I didn't see many dry eyes. A lot were openly weeping and dabbing at their eyes—as was I. In fact, I have a difficult time talking about it even now.

When I reached the parking lot, I found that someone had parked behind my car, blocking the way out. At the moment, I felt rotten and just wanted to be somewhere else. But an usher spotted my predicament and said he could locate the driver of the other car. When the driver showed up, he was no better off than I—all teared up and apologetic.

To show how the ex-players were affected, let me relay a poem which former catcher Rick Dempsey sent to the Oriole Advocates, who gave me permission to read it at their luncheon and later for television stations.

A Tribute to Memorial Stadium

She's the lady in red, she's Baltimore's best
And many a great one has come from her nest;
She gave birth to a thousand, adopted a few,
By the way she loved them, nobody knew.
There was Brooksie and Frank and Booger by name
There was Palmer, McNally, Paulie and the Blade,
Eddie and Flanny and Tippy and Scott,
Dobber and Cuellar, Stanhouse and Stot,
There was Bumbry and Kell, Gary and Lo,
Richie and Dennis, Gus and the Crow.
She made Earl her general and Ripken the Sarge,
And they led her children on a perilous charge,
But when the battles had ended and Octobers subside
There stood the lady in all of her pride.
She's gray now and tired and goes to lay down
With the pennants God gave her to wear as her crown.
Glory and honor will sleep at her feet
For the miracles she gave us on 33rd Street.

I was in Camden Yards the night that Cal Ripken tied Lou Gehrig's streak of 2,130 consecutive games and I was asked to

For the Love of the Game

add some of my comments to the CBS Radio broadcast on the night he broke the record.

As opposed to the quiet dignity of the crowd watching the ex-players at Memorial Stadium's closing, the reaction for Cal's record-breaking game was wild, wonderful, and raucous. I can't imagine any fan who was there ever having had a better experience.

Baseball desperately needed what Cal gave it in 1995 and, unfortunately, he can only do it that one time. For those two nights in Baltimore, I didn't hear anybody complaining about how much money the players made or how little the owners knew about running ballclubs. For two nights, Camden Yards was the place to be and people all over the world had a pretty good idea of what was going on when Cal tied and then broke the record. Bill Ripken, Cal's younger brother who played alongside him at second base for the Orioles from 1987 to 1992 and who would rejoin the Orioles in 1996, was in the crowd for the momentous occasion.

Although I was working with CBS Radio, I had a monitor to follow what was going out on TV. If there's one picture that will stay with me forever, it would be when Cal stood outside the backstop screen and touched the hand of his brother Bill who was standing on the other side. For one sensational moment, they stood face to face, brother to brother, professional to professional.

I thought the changing of those large numbers on the warehouse during the game was an absolutely magnificent way to publicize the streak. When the record was broken and the number "2131" appeared, there was a kind of eruption I had never heard at a ballpark. I'd been around for no-hitters, great World Series wins, and stunning football games such as the Colts overtime win over the New York Giants in 1958, but this was the topper. I'd never witnessed such joyous celebration, excitement, and exultation as I did when "2131" went into the record books (by season's end, the streak had grown to 2153).

Because of the strike baseball was not the fair-haired child you'd like it to be, but for that one moment all was right with the world. The eruption had to be heard in Washington, Philadelphia, and anywhere else around the world where it was carried by radio and television.

Ain't the Beer Cold!

My most enjoyable moment was when I saw pictures of Cal, Sr., and his wife Vi with the other Ripken children in the stands. This was Junior's night and they didn't want to be on the field; but they did join him for the post-game ceremony, along with Cal's wife Kelly and their two small children, Rachel and Ryan. I just had to look at that family and say, "Hot dang, I wouldn't have missed this for the world!"

When the record was officially broken in the fifth inning, the game was held up for 22 minutes for an on-field celebration. It was then that teammates Rafael Palmeiro and Bobby Bonilla shoved a hesitant Cal onto the warning track to start a victory lap.

Cal may have been reluctant at first but once he made it down the right-field side and saw the joy and pride on the faces of the fans, I could almost see from the booth that the tension he had been carrying around for so long was just rolling off him like perspiration from the brow. The pressure and difficulties of recent days had disappeared and he was just a kid at the ballpark having fun, and he had a chance to show his appreciation.

Two guys fell from the seats in center field and Cal retreated momentarily to make sure they were OK, exchanged a couple of "high fives" with them, and continued on. The Orioles in the bullpen were hanging over the fence, waiting for him, and players in the elevated visitors' bullpen applauded as he went past.

Cal stopped and spoke briefly with some fans along the left-field line and exchanged more "high fives". It was sheer fun, something that he was obviously enjoying.

When he went past the applauding umpires, he stopped and shook hands with each of the four, and did the same with many of the California Angels who had moved to the top of the dugout steps. Cal hugged Hall-of-Famer Rod Carew and they exchanged a few words.

It was the kind of night that lovers of baseball cherish and want to relive during the long winter nights as they await the start of spring training. As someone once wrote, baseball starts in the spring when everything else begins to bloom, blossoms in the summer as it fills our afternoons and evenings, and as soon as the

For the Love of the Game

leaves begin to fall and the chilled rains come, it stops and leaves us to face the fall and winter, all alone.

I don't know the origin of those words, which I've heard often, but I can attribute the following excerpts from the "Baseball Is" composition to Greg Hall of Kansas City, Missouri. Greg, a lifelong baseball fan, wanted to pass along his feelings about the sport to his son Shannon, who was five months old and riding in the car with his dad when a news report on the radio announced the start of the strike in 1994.

Baseball Is

Baseball is sitting in your car
On a humid, summer night,
Listening to the play-by-play on the only
    radio that will pick up the game.

Baseball is a voice in a box,
Describing men you've never met,
In a place you've never been,
Doing things you'll never have the
    chance to do.

Baseball is the potential for a no-hitter
    with every National Anthem.

Baseball is 90 feet of anticipation.

Baseball is my dad hollering score
    updates upstairs after mom had
    long ago sent us to bed.

Baseball is a tear rolling down the
    cheek of a child in uniform,
As he watches a thunderstorm wash out
    the day's game.

Ain't the Beer Cold!

Baseball is a scribbled and blotched
    scorecard that can make a 6-4-3
    look like a ballet.

Baseball is imitating every nuance of
    the stance of your favorite player.

Baseball is how I learned my geography.

Baseball is taught by dads to sons in
    hopes that the boy will master the
    game that the man did not.

Baseball is Willie vs. Mickey,
    Gibson vs. Koufax and
    Buddy Biancalana vs. the odds

Baseball links Kansan and Missourian,
    American and Japanese,
    But most of all,
    Father and son.

Baseball is a language of very simple
    words that tell unbelievably magic tales.

Baseball is the foreign sensation you get
    when placing your hand into someone else's glove.

Baseball is the way generations compare
    themselves and their idols.

Baseball is a breast pocket bulging with
    a transistor radio.

Baseball is the reason there are
    transistor radios.

For the Love of the Game

Baseball is a dream that you never
    really give up on.

Baseball is precious.
Baseball is timeless.
Baseball is forever.

After reading such poignant lines I feel like rejoicing, and the only meaningful words I could add would be in the form of a toast:

AIN'T THE BEER COLD!